Ancient Swordplay

The Revival of Elizabethan Fencing in Victorian London

By Tony Wolf

Freelance Academy Press, Inc.
www.FreelanceAcademyPress.com

Cover/Title Page Image: "The Sword and Dagger Fight" – Egerton Castle (right) demonstrates "ancient swordplay" at a meeting of the Kernoozers Club. Illustration by Harry Furniss for M.H. Spielmann's article, "Glimpses of Artist-Life VII: The Kernoozers Club." *The Magazine of Art*, Vol. 12. London, Cassell and Company.

Freelance Academy Press, Inc., Wheaton, IL 60189
www.freelanceacademypress.com

Printed in the United States of America
by Publishers' Graphics

21 20 19 18 17 16 15 14 13 12 1 2 3 4 5

ISBN 978-0-9825911-8-5

Library of Congress Control Number: 2011932932

Table of Contents

A Note on the Illustrations

In preparing this book the author has searched relentlessly through old newspapers, magazines, journals and play bills, many of them well over a century old. Many were never printed on anything sturdier than newsprint; others have been ravaged by time and exist only in old photocopies, or in extremely delicate condition. Every effort has been made to improve their resolution and print them at as high a quality as possible.

However, to make those meritorious images that could not be made print-worthy available to as wide an audience as possible, they will be found digitally on the publisher's website: http://www.freelanceacademypress.com/articles.aspx

Foreword

Historical martial arts reward their practitioners in many ways: to name only a few, entertainment, comradeship, intellectual stimulation, and all the benefits attendant on vigorous exercise. In addition they provide another rich source of fascination and pleasure that is not quite so easy to sum up in a couple of words. I refer to the feeling, commonly savored by those who apply their minds and bodies to the rediscovery of these ancient systems, of direct physical continuity with the past. A tourist entering the nave of a medieval cathedral can feel some of what its ancient parishioners felt as their feet trod the same stones. A modern chorister singing a part in a Renaissance motet partakes in a sort of communion with singers who intoned the same notes five hundred years ago. And a swordsman poring over a digital scan of a six-hundred-year-old fencing manual, working through a series of attacks and counterattacks with a partner, will occasionally feel something akin to an electric shock when suddenly the connection is made and a spark jumps the gap. Centuries ago, two master swordsmen stood in a courtyard, doing precisely what my partner and I are doing now, holding the pose for a few moments, perhaps, as an artist captured them in a few rough but deft strokes of a quill on fresh parchment. This book has lain in dark places through all of the rising and falling of kingdoms and empires, the wars and revolutions, dark times and enlightenments since then, and now here we are in a gymnasium in

Chicago or a park in Vancouver staring at a copy of that book and translating those pen-strokes into living bodies and movements again, *and it all works*. It works because, for all of the changes that have occurred since that quill stroked across that sheepskin—for all of the cultural shifts that made those ancient swordsmen as culturally different from us as Maori are from Michiganders—we are still humans, living in the same bodies with the same powers and weaknesses, the same faculties of perception, impelled by the same drives and inhibited by the same fears.

This sense of uncanny continuity with the past is now enriched even further by Tony Wolf's *Ancient Swordplay,* which introduces the modern historical swordplay community to its older brothers and sisters of the Victorian age.

It has long been understood that the Victorians had martial arts of their own, stick fighting being one example. And research conducted during the last decade or so by Mr. Wolf and his colleagues has established that they were keen on importing (to them) outlandish martial arts such as jiujitsu. These facts have become widely understood among the historical martial arts community. The new, and fascinating, information conveyed in *Ancient Swordplay* is that the same people launched a thorough, vigorous, and passionate revival of martial traditions that were *to them* archaic, and that in doing so they ventured down many of the same paths that are being re-discovered and re-explored in the early 21st century. The modern swordfighter, learning a new technique from the works of the Elizabethan master George Silver, is communing not only with Silver (1560s–1620s) but with Alfred Hutton (1839–1910) who *also* stumbled upon Silver and re-learnt the same techniques at the dawn of the Twentieth Century.

To describe this book's contents in any further detail would be to delay the reader's enjoyment, and so I invite anyone who has read this far to turn the page and dive into this story. Even those who have no familiarity with, or interest in, the modern-day revival of ancient martial arts should find it an engaging portrait of some of the lesser-known characters, societies, and trends of the late Victorian age, and might even be moved to make contact with persons in their own towns who are today carrying the torch that was lit a century and a half ago by the likes of Richard Francis Burton and Alfred Hutton. Those who are already busying themselves in such arts will be delighted to read tales of their illustrious forebears, while perhaps coming away from this book's final chapter with food for thought on how to prevent the current revival from fading out as its first wave of practitioners recedes into history and perhaps become the subject matter of future books like this one.

NEAL STEPHENSON
Seattle, October 2011

Preface

> "Curiously enough, it is in England (the country which for so long has neglected the systematic practice of this fascinating sport) that the true character of ancient sword-play, and its evolution towards the highly perfect art which we now call fencing, was first elucidated.
>
> "Investigation of the doctrine of ancient masters of fence and bibliographic compilation of fencing works were things naturally bound to go hand in hand; both are virtually branches of what is now becoming the fashion to speak of as Kernoozing. And this investigation (at least in a really systematic manner) belongs to quite modern times."
>
> – Carl Albert Thimm,
> *A Complete Bibliography of Fencing and Duelling*, 1896

This book details the revival of "ancient," especially Elizabethan, swordplay during the late 19th century, focusing upon the work of two Englishmen, Egerton Castle and Alfred Hutton, who were jointly responsible for much of that revival. Their efforts presaged those of the modern Historical European martial arts movement, whose more immediate origins are usually traced to the 1970s. Throughout, I have concentrated on the systematic, technical reconstruction of ancient swordplay, as distinct from both purely academic efforts, such as the republication of antique fencing treatises, and the incidental or anachronistic use of historical weapons in theatre and pageantry. However, during the late Victorian era, revived ancient swordplay found practical expression in a wide variety of formats, including classes, educational exhibitions, theatrical fight choreography, formal lectures, and the publication of books and essays, examples of which are all duly noted.

The late-Victorian revival of Elizabethan fencing is fairly widely recognized in modern Historical European Martial Arts (HEMA) circles, but is typically treated in a somewhat cavalier fashion, or even dismissed out of hand. I believe that this is due to a confluence of two negative stereotypes. The first is based upon several oft-quoted passages from Egerton Castle's book *Schools and Masters of Fence*, as shall be discussed in the following chapter, and the second is due to a modern perception that the 19th century marked the evolution of European swordsmanship into "mere sport."

While both of these perspectives have bases in fact, they are also incomplete. The more holistic context of the Victorian "ancient swordplay" revival suggests that Hutton and Castle should, in point of fact, be celebrated as true pioneers in this field. As alluded to by their colleague Carl Thimm, they essentially invented (and certainly popularized) the systematic practice of reviving historical fencing systems, and they achieved a level of historical accuracy that has not been exceeded until recent years. The central theme of this book is to examine that revival, as much as possible via their own words and those of their collaborators, critics and audiences.

For all of their efforts, Hutton and Castle did not establish a legacy of historical fencing practice that would survive their own generation; if they had, of course, the modern revival would have been redundant. In the final chapters of this book, I attempt to answer why this was so, and to trace their influence, and in at least one case, their lineage of practice, beyond the First World War and into the following generations of the twentieth century.

Anticipating that many readers will be members of the modern historical fencing community, I hope that you enjoy this journey into the relatively recent past and that you will find kindred spirits in Alfred Hutton, Egerton Castle and their colleagues. In so many ways, they were just like us.

TONY WOLF

Amantea, Italy, September 2009

Acknowledgements

I would like to thank Steve Hick, Professor Daniel Marciano, Michel Hewer, Jerome Faure, Laura Erickson, Manuel Valle, Fabrice Cognot, Alex Kiermayer and Maxime Chouinard for their kind assistance in researching the world of "ancient swordplay"; my editors, Greg Mele and Tom Leoni, for their top-notch work in developing the manuscript for publication; Neal Stephenson, for his contribution of a Foreword; my parents, Michael and Jill, for their support; my son Josh, for playing along over two decades' worth of applied hoplological research; and my wife, Kathrynne, for everything.

Egerton Castle poses with rapier and dagger for the original frontispiece of *Schools and Masters of Fence* (1884)

Chapter 1

Egerton Castle

The year was 1878. The acclaimed British actor/director Henry Irving had revived his famous production of *Hamlet* for London's Lyceum Theatre, with himself in the title role. Among the most lauded scenes in what was widely held to be a masterful revival was the fencing match between Hamlet and Laertes in the final act:

> HAMLET – Come, for the third, Laertes: you but dally;
> I pray you, pass with your best violence; I am afeard you make a wanton of me.
>
> LAERTES – Say you so? Come on.
>
> *They play*
>
> OSRIC – Nothing, neither way.
>
> LAERTES – Have at you now!
>
> *LAERTES wounds HAMLET; then in scuffling, they change rapiers, and HAMLET wounds LAERTES*
>
> KING CLAUDIUS – Part them; they are incensed.
>
> HAMLET – Nay, come, again!

Seated in the Lyceum audience one evening, enraptured most particularly by the cut and thrust of the rapiers, was a young university student named Egerton Castle. So inspired was he that, over the next three decades, Castle would become instrumental in the revival of Elizabethan fencing.

Anthony Egerton Castle was born in London on the 12th of March in the year 1858. His father, Arthur Michael Castle, was heir to a substantial fortune via the burgeoning newspaper industry and he fared widely throughout the European continent on business and for pleasure. He made a frequent travelling companion of his son, introducing young Egerton to artists, musicians and men of letters, including Donizetti and Verdi, Liszt and Rossini, Gounod, Alexandre Dumas, Robert Browning, and many other notables.

Egerton was naturally delicate, and his father had instituted a rather Spartan regime of exercises to develop his constitution and physique. These included long hiking tours through German forests and on the banks of the Mediterranean Sea, as well as wrestling, sea rowing, gymnastics, riding, boxing and the fundamentals of fencing. He was also a voracious reader of swashbuckling historical romances, later claiming that "the creators of D'Artagnan, of Admirable Crichton, and of Bussy d'Amboise, made me a swordsman." At fifteen years of age, when he graduated from the Lycée Condorcet in Paris, Egerton was already a tall, strapping young man. He was fluent in Spanish, German, French and Italian as well as English, with a thorough working knowledge of Latin and Greek.

Settling in England at the age of eighteen, he had become, as described by a journalist in 1902, "almost a stranger to his own country; intensely patriotic, but viewing things in the attitude of a keen yet sympathetic observer." Two years of private tutoring followed, then matriculation at the University of Glasgow, where his studies included chemical philosophy and practical physics. Returning to London Egerton Castle enrolled first at King's College, before winning a science scholarship to Trinity College, Cambridge. He later referred to his four years at Cambridge as "a fragrant chapter in my life"; at the time, he planned to pursue a professorship.

However, due perhaps to his father's eclectic intellectual, cultural and physical training regimen, Castle was of an active as well as scholarly temperament. In 1878, inspired by Henry Irving's stage swordplay as Hamlet, he began to formally study fencing, building upon the boyhood lessons arranged for him by his father and fuelled by his ongoing affection for the adventures of D'Artagnon. Egerton competed in a tournament at Cambridge, winning a prize donated by Angelo's famed fencing school in London.

In 1880, seeking ever more robust adventures, Castle joined Sandhurst Military Academy, where he gained a commission as a cavalry officer in a West Indian regiment.He was promoted twice within two years and, in 1882, won a gold medal in swordsmanship as a competitor in the prestigious Royal Tournament and Assault at Arms, which was a national competition in all manner of soldierly skills. He became a captain of the Royal Engineer Militia and there supplemented his education with courses in submarine mining at Chatham and Gosport. It was also in that year that Castle was particularly impressed by an essay written by the esteemed barrister, Sir Frederick Pollock, on *The Forms and History of the Sword.*

Failing to secure a placement in his preferred regiment, Castle eventually gave up his commission and found himself in search of a profession, and indeed, a life outside either formal military or academic disciplines. He initially chose law, enrolling for a short time at the Inner Temple, but he quickly found that he had little patience for the subject. He then flirted with the idea of becoming a professional "Pursuivant of Arms," and enrolled for a time in the Herald's College. However, he found that while his prior education was a superb preparation for a career in Heraldry, he was increasingly drawn to writing on other, more personally engaging topics.

In 1883 Castle wooed and then married a beautiful and brilliant young Irish lady named Agnes Sweetman, and the two of them settled into a professional and personal collaboration that was to last the rest of their lives. Castle had already written a number of well-received articles on various topics, but upon marrying Agnes, who also had literary ambitions, he committed himself to a working life as a professional author and began to search for a topic that would establish him in that sphere.

At about the same time, Castle attended a lecture on swords and swordplay by Sir Frederick Pollock, whose essay had remained fresh in his memory. During the lecture, Pollock commented that a full account of the development of fencing would require an entire book, not a simple discourse, and that such a book had not yet been written. Perhaps co-incidentally, in 1882 a French fencer and bibliophile, M. Arsene Vigeant, did produce such a work, entitled *La Bibliographie de l'Escrime Ancienne et Moderne*. As a survey of swordplay texts it was met with great enthusiasm within the fencing community, although it was criticized for missing some important works, especially those written in languages other than French.

Castle's mounting enthusiasm for the subject of fencing was further spurred by the announcement that the famed explorer, ethnologist and linguistic scholar Captain Richard Burton, who was one of Castle's personal heroes, was planning a magnum opus on the history and development of the sword itself, rather than the systems of its use. It seemed that an engaging topic had found the young writer.

Thus, Egerton Castle's first major publication, produced in something of a youthful fervour, was the monumental *Schools and Masters of Fence* (1884), a comprehensive history tracing the development of European swordsmanship from the Middle Ages to Castle's own era. So important was this book that, to this day, it is one of the most often-quoted works on historical swordsmanship. However, with the advantage of an additional century-and-a-half of research, with scores of ancient fencing treatises having been discovered in libraries and private collections, and with a detachment from the "evolutionary" culture that permeated late-Victorian thought, we are in the position to analyze *Schools and Masters,* itself, as a historical work.

Let us address the most critical issue first. Some of Castle's assertions in *Schools and Masters* have been widely criticized within the modern historical fencing movement. He appears to have accepted Pollock's assumption of a linear evolution in the design of swords, and to have elaborated that assumption into his critique of earlier systems and theories of swordplay. Especially self-damning, from the perspective of current hoplological scholarship, are Castle's rather dismissive comments on the "rough and undisciplined swordsmanship" of the Middle Ages, and similar remarks that pepper the early chapters of his book:

> "The rough untutored fighting of the Middle Ages represented faithfully the reign of brute force in social life as well as in politics. The stoutest arm and the weightiest sword won the day, even as did the sturdiest baron or the most warlike king. Those were the days of crushing blows with mace or glaive,

> when a knight's superiority in action depended upon his power of wearing heavier armor and dealing heavier blows than his neighbour, when strength was lauded more than skill, and minstrels sang of enchanted blades that nought could break."

To the modern critic, who has the advantage of over a century of hindsight, it is worth bearing in mind that Egerton Castle was only twenty-six years old when *Schools and Masters* was first published. As an independently wealthy, multi-lingual scholar in several disciplines who was also a passionate fencer, he was almost uniquely well qualified to write a pan-European history of swordsmanship. Importantly, however, it appears that his research for *Schools and Masters of Fence* did not include close study of some of the key treatises that clearly demonstrate the advanced science of, for example, the play of the two-handed sword during the 15th and the early 16th centuries.

Castle saw fencing as both a beautiful art and an exacting science; it seems that, at this time, he was unable to reconcile "his" fencing with what he knew of the earliest styles, especially the use of the two-handed sword in armoured combat and most especially the combination of cut and thrust fencing with grappling techniques.

As we shall see, Castle later came to recognize the practical utility of such skills as "wrestling at the sword," but in 1884 he clearly saw the "perfection" of academic fencing in his own era as owing its origins to the rapier-play of Camillo Agrippa. Acknowledging these limitations in the light of more recent scholarship, we should evaluate Castle based on the impact of his work on the practical reconstruction of "ancient swordplay" in late-Victorian England.

Given its highly specialized subject matter and the fact that, in 1884, Castle himself had no particular reputation either as a historian, swordsman nor as an author, *Schools and Masters of Fence* was quite extraordinarily successful. Critics called it "a treasure," "both admirable in execution and highly readable."

Unauthorized translations quickly appeared in France, Germany, Italy and Holland; the latter pirated version did not even offer credit in the form of Castle's name on the title page. Unlawful distribution issues aside, the book was popular and impressive enough that on its strength, two years later, Castle found himself elected to the French Académie d'Armes. The Academie was a then-recently re-founded institution whose original model dated back to the sixteenth century. Egerton Castle's election was a high honour, indeed, for an English scholar/amateur fencer who was still in his twenties.

It seems highly likely that, at some stage of his research for *Schools and Masters* or perhaps even earlier, Castle must have begun practical experiments with various historical weapons and fighting styles. Perhaps some insight into this process is available from the following passage, excerpted from one of his novels:

> "And so you are a good swordsman. I am glad of that," repeated Fargus musingly, as they wound their way toward the school. "But how do you come to be a fencer?" he went on, glancing with some pride at the well set-up figure by his side. "Most of your countrymen, if I am not mistaken, now look upon scientific fencing as an un-English, not to say Frenchified, pursuit."
>
> "That is a John Bullish sort of idea which, I am glad to say, is fast disappearing from the army. In olden days we had the best broadswordsmen in Europe, and I assure you we have still a fair number of such. With me sword-play of every description has always been a special taste; I began to cultivate the noble science at the early age of twelve. It came about in this way. I must tell you that I never knew my father, and that my mother died at my birth. She was Spanish, and I was brought up by my Spanish grandparents, partly at Seville, where I was born, partly in an old, very dilapidated family place they had, near Ronda—a sort of strong-house, half castle, half farm, where we used to pass the summer. There was a large loft in one of the towers of this last, where old furniture and rubbish of all kinds, rusty odds and ends of arms and armor, blackened pictures and torn books, were stuffed away—a favorite haunt of mine, whither one day my grandfather traced me unawares, to find me practicing by myself, a broken 'brown rapier' in one

> hand and in the other a battered book of fence of the days of Philip IV. It seems he watched me with delight, as I pinked and hacked the back of a fine old Cordova leather armchair in the true orthodox style as laid down in the *Book of the Sword's Splendor*. And the old man was so pleased with what he considered an innate taste for gentlemanly accomplishments, that he engaged, the very next week, a man from Seville to come and give me lessons of 'dexterity.' Dear old unsophisticated grandfather!"
>
> – Egerton Castle,
> *Consequences: A Novel*, pp. 186–7

It is a scant few years after the publication of *Schools and Masters* that the record reveals the practice of revived "ancient swordplay" in England; but before we investigate those reports, it is necessary to introduce a man who should actually need no introduction to most readers interested in historical swordsmanship. This was Castle's longtime collaborator and friend, a formidable swordsman and no mean antiquarian in his own right: the redoubtable Captain Alfred Hutton.

Captain Alfred Hutton poses with rapier, circa 1898

Chapter 2

Alfred Hutton

Hutton was nearly twenty years senior to Egerton Castle. He was born in the English town of Beverley on March 10th, 1839, the eleventh and youngest child of Henry William and Marianne Hutton.

Alfred started fencing at the age of twelve in the London *ecole d'armes* of Henry Angelo, the younger; his father had studied there with Henry's father. Alfred later confessed that he had been bullied by other boys at school, and was initially drawn to fencing as a potential method of self defence in which strength mattered less than dexterity.

Hutton matriculated at University College, Oxford in 1857, but left without graduating to join the 75th (Cameron) Highanders in 1859. He immediately proved his mettle when, as a raw Ensign, he was awoken one night by a party of junior officers preparing for the traditional "ragging" or hazing of the new recruit.

> "Captain Dash, you are, I believe, the senior officer present in this room?" Ensign Hutton enquired.
>
> "Yes, young shaver, I am—what of it?" Dash replied.
>
> "Oh, nothing. I merely wish to say that if I have to get out of bed, you, Captain Dash, as the senior officer, will be the first of the party to go over the banisters."

No ragging took place that night.

On his arrival at the Perth depot, Hutton encountered a Scottish Sergeant-Major whose habit was to challenge newcomers to friendly bouts of fencing. Hutton won the first bout using a sabre against the Sergeant's rifle-bayonet and then disarmed his opponent in the second contest, for which they had swapped weapons; the Sergeant declined a third bout at sabre vs. sabre and Hutton was acclaimed as the depot's new champion-at-arms.

When Hutton transferred to his regiment's base he was asked by his commanding officer, Colonel Hodgson, to organize a regimental fencing school. In 1862 Hutton produced his first book on fencing, which was entitled *Swordsmanship,* as a manual for the Cameron Fencing Club.

Two years later, Hutton exchanged into the 7th Hussars and then into the 1st (King's) Dragoon guards. He popularized the practice of fencing in every regiment to which he became attached, to the extent that he was later nicknamed "the father of army fencing."

In early 1865 he contracted a tropical illness and was invalided home to England. Upon his recovery, Hutton retained his particular enthusiasm for fencing, becoming the pupil and friend of William McTurk, who had taken over teaching at the Salle d'Angelo in St. James's Street. The following year, Hutton also became a member of the London Fencing Club. Still holding his commission, he was gazetted Captain on September 30, 1868, and retired from service in 1873. Now a gentleman of leisure, Hutton could indulge his passions. The following year he became one of the founders of the Central London Throat and Ear Hospital, and remained the chairman of that institution's Board of Directors for the next thirty years. Aside from his philanthropic work, Hutton devoted himself largely to the study of fencing with the foil, sabre and bayonet. He also accumulated an impressive collection of antique arms and fencing books.

The collaboration between Alfred Hutton and Egerton Castle was probably as inevitable as it was undoubtedly profitable. Although we have no record of their first meeting, it seems likely that the two men had met shortly after Henry Irving's production of *Hamlet,* which had made such an impression on the young Castle, for, as was mentioned by Professor John Dover Wilson in 1934:

> "I am told by fencers who remember Irving's performance at the Lyceum in 1878, the scene was played under the direction of Alfred Hutton, the well-known and learned fencer."
>
> – *The Manuscript of Shakespeare's 'Hamlet'*

It is probable that Castle and Hutton worked together on the reconstruction of various ancient methods of swordplay during the early 1880s. In the introduction to *Schools and Masters,* Castle mentions that "some time ago," Hutton had leant him "a magnificent collection of books treating of the sword and its use, ranging in date from the early 16th century to the present day." Castle's dedication may also be revealing:

> "Inscribed to Baron de Cosson and captain A. Hutton, in recollection of many pleasant hours spent, with the former among old books and old arms, with the latter in the fencing room, foil in hand."

Thus, in the collaboration between Castle and Hutton, informed and inspired by Sir Richard Burton, Sir Frederick Pollock, and Sir Henry Irving, was formed a nascent community of fencing antiquarians. In the next chapter we shall peek through the curtains of history and enjoy a glimpse of this association of highly educated, affluent and ambitious gentlemen, discussing ancient swords and swordplay in the opulent, candle-lit club rooms of Victorian London.

We Seek For This
CLUB

Chapter 3

The Kernoozers Club

Castle's dedication to the Baron de Cosson is particularly interesting. Charles Alexander, Baron de Cosson was a near contemporary of Alfred Hutton's, and although not a swordsman himself in the practical sense, he was an inveterate collector of antique arms and armour. In 1881, de Cosson had co-founded, and became president of, a private gentlemen's club whose membership was restricted to twenty men, including a number of famous artists and well-connected antiquarians. All were strictly amateur enthusiasts; professional involvement in auctioneering, the commercial sale of antiques and so-on barred any applicant from joining the club, which was devoted to the location, study and preservation of ancient weapons and suits of armour. This select clique was known as the Kernoozers Club.

The name was a humorous travesty of the word connoisseur, in honor of a comment by a man then well-known and respected in artistic circles, who, in his youth, had earned his living by posing as a model for some of the best painters of the day. Over the years he had come by an extensive and detailed knowledge of art and artists, and he had procured for his son a splendid artistic and general education, although he himself remained largely illiterate. One day a Christie's auctioneer sought him out for a sound opinion on an unusual piece of armor. "Here, my friend," he said; "say frankly—what do you think of this suit?" "Well," responded the other, with his usual candour, "'taint no use asking me anythink about armour and sech-like. As the Frenchman says, I'm no *kernoozer*."

The word kernoozer, occasionally spelled "kerneuzer," thereafter became something of a light-hearted code-word among Club members, used to describe various attitudes and practices relating to the study of ancient armature ("I kernoozled a fine helmet the other day," etc.) It was used both as a verb and a substantive, generally signifying a pleasant confabulation on technical matters of interest to Club members, "leavened with cold meats and strong and effervescent drinks." By the 1890s, "kernoozing" had also come to describe the practice of historical fencing based on antique treatises and manuscripts.

The Club's founding charter read, in part:

> "The Kernoozers Club is formed for the purpose of promoting friendly intercourse between Gentlemen who study or collect Ancient Armour and Arms, and will be composed only of those who either possess collections of arms and armour or who have written some published work on the subject."

The Club's co-founder and frequent vice-president had been John Seymour Lucas (1849–1923), a member of the Royal Academy, the Institute of Painters in Watercolours, and a Fellow of the Society of Antiquaries. His interest in arms and armour was initially spurred by a desire for detailed historical accuracy in his paintings, a typical motivation of many Kernoozers, at least initially. As the Club matured, however, its enthusiasms expanded into other areas of antiquarianism, and a revision of the charter in 1905 stated that:

> "The Kernoozers Club is formed for the purpose of promoting friendly intercourse between Gentlemen who collect Arms and Armour, Costumes, Furniture, and other Antiquities, as well as to encourage the study thereof, and shall be composed of those who possess collections or who have written or published some work on the subjects, or who are Associates, Fellows, or Members of one of the Royal Art or Antiquarian Societies."

For Victorian and Edwardian gentlemen, membership in at least one well-regarded club was virtually a pre-requisite to upper and middle-class respectability. It also offered social and professional networking opportunities and the chance to indulge one's hobbies with like-minded fellows. That said, the minutes and scrap-books of the Kernoozers Club, which are presently held by the British Library, suggest an underlying sense of almost boyish enthusiasm for their subject; many members chose to be photographed for the Club archives wearing historical costume or armor and bearing antique weapons triumphantly aloft.

Although the Kernoozers were not precisely a "secret society," they *were* exclusive and so their meetings were not typically open either to reporters or to the general public. This leant their activities a certain esoteric flavor, comparable to that of Freemasonry, and it is evident that this aura of mystery was very much cultivated and enjoyed by the members of the Club. Thus, very few detailed accounts of their activities were ever made public. However, the atmosphere of a typical late-night Kernoozer Club meeting was described in an article written by M.H. Spielmann for *The Magazine of Art* in October of 1889.

> "...when all the expected guests have arrived they sit around in an informal crescent, and the Vice-President—on this occasion Mr. Seymour Lucas, F.S.A., A.R.A.—reads a paper in a conversational but an earnest tone. His manner appears what might be called smilingly combative, for he is evidently talking with the weight of conviction upon him, and his words are the outcome of long and diligent research. Moreover, the subject of his little discourse, which happily meets with the entire approbation of the assembly, is based upon a great and valuable *trouvaille* of his own—a mighty two-handed sword, some four to five feet in length, belonging to the thirteenth century, which has been rescued by him from the ignorant care of some Midland bucolic, and which, from the 'marks" of its Galas upon it and other internal as well as external evidence, would appear to have been the Joyeuse of King John himself. A 'state sword' it certainly was

"Then follows a desultory conversation upon the weapon; and the quillons, and the pommel, and the blade of the doughty *espadon* are all descanted upon with eagerness, while the methods of its use are illustrated by Mr. Egerton Castle, the champion swordsman of the club. Attention is now devoted to all the other objects in turn with a quite curious absence of jealousy on the part of the collectors; the relish and indomitable persistence with which men of the school will discuss and re-discuss them is one of the most astonishing characteristics of the clan. At length the solleret and mail-shirt is talked out for a time, and the singing and playing by professional musicians of renown add softness to the pipe and quality to the liquor ... and then in knots of two or three we descend, still warmly continuing or listening to the discussion, to the supper-room below, which has been stocked strictly in accordance with the club injunctions.

"Soon the small hours come and go, and then cries are raised for the 'Punch-bowl,' the song the host is famous for, and which he sings to perfection. So filling a glass of toddy (just to keep up the illusion), he sends the drinking-song carolling forth from his musical throat and lips. By this time all the early-risers have left, and just as young Nick is inwardly yearning for bed, a couple of youngsters, more lively than the rest, make a raid on the fine hanging suits of armour and weapons, and deaf to the polite entreaties of the distracted owner, proceed to gird them on. The hint is sufficient for the others. They run to the cassoni, and drag out their beautiful contents, which they don, irrespective of date and custom, until they appear as masqueraders more incoherent and eccentric than the wildest dreams of Mme. Tussaud's could suggest."

A more prosaic account is offered in this passage, excerpted from a 1908 biography of the artist John Pettie:

> "Entertainment for the evening was provided by the member at whose house the monthly meeting was held. It was a strict regulation that the fare should be of the simplest kind—roast beef, cheese, beer, claret, pipes, tobacco, whisky, and nothing more. Amid the wreaths of smoke they held debate on historical dress and fine armour, on casque and chanfron, solleret and cuisse. Various 'kernoozers' brought the pieces of armour which they had acquired during the month; these were discussed, and sometimes a paper was read. On a special visitors' night, Mr. Egerton Castle and another member would explain feats of swordsmanship or illustrate a 'sword-and-dagger fight.' Pettie was often present, and besides enjoying the social character of the meetings, got many a wrinkle as to weapons and their uses."
>
> – Martin Hardie, *John Pettie, R.A., H.R.S.A.*, 1908

Another Kernoozer rule—stringently insisted upon and loyally subscribed to—was that no member should keep a "kernoozing" secret from the rest of the Club. By that means, "common good feeling was placed on a firm basis, and a sense of intersecurity and material advancement was realised."

Naturally, as a coterie of Victorian gentlemen whose interests tended towards Medieval romance, the Kernoozers were a courteous society. There is a record of one of their meetings which happened to be convened at the home of a Hampstead artist who was both deaf and mute, and whose wife had that night taken to bed early to recover from a cold.

> "And then comes a very pretty act of consideration on the part of the guests. After the meal is finished and a toast or two proposed and acknowledged, it is suggested that the host should be pledged, and that the singing of 'For he's a jolly good fellow' should wind up the proceedings. But it is remembered that the lady of the house is in ill-health, so that, rather than rob the host of the intended honour, the song is sung *in dumb*

> *show,* with every accompaniment of rollicking joviality. So our chairman is pleased, his wife is undisturbed, and we, though rather ashamed of our innocent deception, feel that we have performed a pleasant duty. From that moment the evening degenerates, or melts, so to speak, into the ordinary smoking-evening, and, the subject being relegated for the time, we revert to old Bohemian habits and Bohemian instincts, and, whiling away the night in good-fellowship, we scarce reach our homes before daylight doth appear."

As well as their monthly meetings, the Kernoozers made annual field-trips, sending scouting parties to ferret out, catalog and study obscure armaments stored in ancient univerities, mansions and cathedrals. The owners or curators of these items were occasionally disappointed to learn that items in their collections were forgeries—or perhaps "fakes" would be a better term, in that all armor is forged—but were more often grateful when the Kernoozer scouts were able to advise them on more secure storage, more artful display, or more historically accurate groupings.

The famous Captain Richard Burton, Egerton Castle and both Frederick and Walter Pollock were all members of the Kernoozers Club, the Pollock brothers and, especially, Burton being eminently well qualified to have partnered Castle in ad hoc demonstrations of swordsmanship. Here is an account of one such demonstration, performed on a rare "visitors' night" at the Kernoozer Club:

> "Mr. Castle, who is attired in a becoming fencing suit of black cord, is called upon to give us a lecture on the popular subject of the use of the sword for the delectation of 'the strangers' (i.e., the visitors). This he does in an informal manner, while those to whom he especially addresses himself strain forward in breathless interest. He speaks to us of the sword and how it grew in succeeding ages and changed its form to

meet new attacks and to permit of new parries; of the quaint phraseology of fencers in Elizabethan and Cavalier days; of how the habits of fence had "evoluted"; how the two-handed sword diminished little by little; how two swords, one in each hand, became the fashion, then one sword with the dagger in the left hand, and then the cloak replacing the dagger. Here is a sentence or two of his address, which was finally illustrated by passages of arms between himself and Mr. Walter Pollock.

"'The rapier—the transition weapon between the sturdy old knightly sword, capable of cracking armour, and the small, or court sword (the dueling weapon of later days)—came into fashion, together with the Italian or Spanish 'Caballero' mannerism, during the latter half of the sixteenth century. It remained the gentle weapon (in opposition to the popular broadsword) until the Parliamentary sword period. After the Restoration the light, triangular, French sword came in, again with foreign mannerism—but French this time. Since then the sword, being no longer a military weapon, became slenderer and lighter until it assumed the bodkin proportion we see in the court sword. The most picturesque period of fencing is that which Mr. Pollock and I will presently illustrate—the Elizabethan. All the outlandish terms used in this mysterious art had the grandiloquent Italian or Spanish character, till there was a perfect infatuation for the fantastical phraseology introduced by followers of Carranza and Saviolo into their daily conversation and intercourse. Even Shakespeare was bitten with it, as *Romeo and Juliet*, *The Merry Wives of Windsor* and *Hamlet* can prove.'

"Then comes the duel by sword and dagger between the two swordsmen, the grace of Mr. Castle and the wary energy and watchfulness of his antagonist being in strong contrast. Every clever stroke, every palpable hit was loudly applauded. The fight was just such a one as was in vogue in Hamlet's time—not the scorpion rapier fence such as Mr. Irving and actors of every grade are content to acquire from the nearest fencing master,

> oblivious to all facts of history—but the desperate and bloody 'sword and dagger fight.' Herein, doubtless, may be found the explanation of the changing of the swords just prior to the death scene in 'Hamlet'—an act which seems hitherto to have puzzled commentator and actor alike. But, as a matter of fact, the interlocking of sword and dagger is a matter of constant occurrence, as our kernoozing belligerents prove. The splendid display of swordsmanship comes to an end by Mr. Castle, who had lost his sword, darting in with lightning rapidity, closing with his adversary, and finishing him off by play (?) of dagger.
>
> "Such, in fine, is the Kernoozers Club, and such it will probably long remain, for similar societies are in process of formation in Paris and Madrid, and it is gradually invading the Society of Antiquaries and making good its title to being the armour-club *par excellence* of the world. In this conviction we slowly leave the scene of the realistic fight and we make our way into the cool, dark street, the clash of steel and Mercutio's cry still ringing in our ears; 'Ah! The immortal passado! The punta reversa! The Hay!'"

Castle himself made several cryptic references to the Club in his *English Book-Plates,* a comprehensive study on the symbolism and aesthetics of personalized book-plates. One of his own plates, designed by his wife Agnes, featured a picture representing:

> "... the Inner Sanctum of that sublimely confident expositor of the 'philosophy of arms,' Master Girard Thibault of Antwerp, who flourished in the days of the 'Three Musketeers'—that dread room where, with the help of diagrams, logical, anatomical, and geometrical, the author of that astounding work, L'Academie de L'Espee professed to teach any number of ineluctable and infallibly mortal strokes."
>
> – Egerton Castle, *English Book-Plates,* 1892

Drawn as if carved into a wooden beam over Thibault's head is the Kernoozers Club motto, *nostrum de armis quaerere,* "it is our business to investigate matters of arms"—and the sentiment at the bottom of the plate reads *Qui porte espee porte paix*—"who bears the sword, bears peace." But investigation was not the only arms-related pursuit of the eager young men who attended the Kernoozers Club. These were also men of action. And for some of their number, action meant not only fencing, but also demonstrating what they knew in the form of exhibitions, which we will explore in the next chapters.

"Assault at Arms with Quarterstaff," *Illustrated London News* (March 26, 1870).

Chapter 4

Early Revivals and Grand Assaults-at-Arms

Exhibitions of historical fencing as semi-theatrical academic diversions (as distinct from theatrical fencing in plays, per se) appear to have caught on at the international level during the late 1880s. There were some precedents, though, including the long European tradition of "historical military pageantry" such as elaborate re-enactments of medieval tournaments. These tournaments were undoubtedly among the most spectacular manifestations of the Gothic Revival that had swept throughout Europe from the 1770s. Perhaps the grandest of them took place in 1837, when Archibald Montgomerie, the 13th Earl of Eglinton, poured a truly staggering sum of money into staging a "Medieval Joust and Revel" at his family's castle and lands near Kilwinning in Scotland. The "knights" who competed were all members of the aristocracy; indeed, no-one else could have afforded to take part, as entrants were required to provide their own armour, weapons, horses and attendants.

The Eglinton Tournament is often recalled as one of the most glorious and infamous follies of the 19th century. Despite many months of preparation, the Tournament was drastically ill-equipped to cope with the enormous crowds who flooded into Kilwinning to witness the spectacle. Roads were blocked by carriage-traffic for miles around and many eager attendees were forced to abandon their coaches and walk to Eglinton Castle. Then, tragically, as the Tournament got underway, a freakishly torrential and prolonged downpour resulted in the "knights" and their mounts struggling through mud and sleet, all but invisible to their audience. Still, the Eglinton Tournament struck a sympathetic chord in the Victorian imagination. The event served to whet the public's appetite for medieval martial spectacle, and this was partly appeased by a theatrical "Tournament and Siege" produced at Astley's Amphitheatre in London a few weeks later.

On a much smaller scale, as early as the 1820s, exhibitions of mock-gladiatorial combat had been staged in French "pleasure gardens" for the amusement of family audiences:

> "New Sport—A new species of entertainment, entitled Les Jeux Eleusi (The Eleusian Games), has recently been produced at the Tivoli Gardens in Paris. It consists of an animated representation of the festivals in honour of Ceres, which were celebrated by the inhabitants of Eleusis in Attica, and which probably first inspired our ancestors with their taste for tilts and tournaments. The first part of the performance consists of a combat of gladiators, armed with swords and shields. Next appear two combatants, both in the character of Hercules, who fight with admirable spirit for the space of ten minutes, and the victor is crowned with a wreath of laurels."
>
> – *The London Literary Gazette and Journal of Belles Lettres, Arts, Sciences, Etc.,* 1820

Unfortunately, there appear to be no records as to whether the gladiatorial fighting techniques featured in these displays were based on any detailed study of historical combat, as represented by carved friezes, paintings on ancient pottery, etc.

The earliest systematic revival of a historical fencing style may have been that associated with a group of Spanish fencers led by the art critic Gregorio Cruzada Villaamil. This revival effort began in Madrid during the late 1850s and is reported to have continued until Villaamil's death in 1884. It was based upon the voluminous and fantastically elaborate printed works of Francisco Lórenz de Rada, compiled during the early 18th century. De Rada's works presented the traditional, aristocratic system of Spanish rapier fencing known as *la Verdadera Destreza* (the "True Skill"). Along with their bibliographic studies, Villaamil and company were also training with Maestro D. Antonio Merino, a disciple of Maestro Cea (also spelled Zea), who had been the last *Maestro Mayor de la Ciencia Philosophica de la Destreza de las Armas* ("Grand Master of the Philosophical Science of the True Dexterity of Arms").

According to *Estudios sobre la grandeza y decadencia de España* ("Studies on the Greatness and Decadence of Spain") (1887), by Felipe Picatoste y Rodríguez:

> "We are pleased to be able to report that the Spanish school (i.e., la Verdadera Destreza) is being reborn, an effort led by the Italians and now spreading throughout all of Europe. Jacob, the first teacher of Paris, follows our old rules; Merignac has established a school of sword and dagger fencing, and Lamarche has written down the theories and rules of Perez de Mendoza. To Spain they have come, in the days in which we write these lines; Franconi, Montini and Garnier, Italian and French, to perfect themselves in the art of the sword with D. Merino Antonio, the disciple of Zea, and last sustainer of this school, which might otherwise have disappeared. This renaissance has, naturally, produced biographical and bibliographical studies, in which the French have committed some inaccuracies, of which works, notably, we must mention those of Vigeau (sic. – Vigeant), who has written the final word on this subject, and who describes Jeronimo de Carranza, the Spanish writer on fencing of the 16th century, as being Portuguese, and says of the work of the Marquess de Rada, who had written two (large) volumes in folio, that it is 'a small work.' In Spain, D. Juan Plastrón has summarized these questions with great success."

Contemporary newspapers record a series of exhibitions presenting Villaamil's reconstructions of "antique" rapier and dagger play for appreciative audiences in Madrid.

The earliest deliberate revival of an archaic fighting style in London appears to have been, not of swordplay, but rather the sport of quarterstaff fencing. Comparatively little is known of the origins of this revival, including (importantly, for present purposes) whether it was based upon direct application of any historical research.

Newspaper reports suggest that an exhibition of French baton (staff) fencing at a military display in Belfast during the year 1851 may have "seeded" the idea of reviving quarterstaff fencing as a competitive sport. Another display of baton fencing was held at an *Assault-at-Arms and Exhibition of Old English Sports* at Saville House in Leicester Square during December of 1853; newspaper reviews commented on the similarity between the contemporary French and ancient English forms of staff fighting. However, it was not until the 1870s that the quarterstaff revival became established, perhaps simply due to a confluence of safety equipment, motivation and opportunity. It may have been fuelled by the renewed, late-Victorian enthusiasm for the tales of Robin Hood.

The *Illustrated London News* of March 26th, 1870 recorded a public "Assault at Arms with Quarterstaff" and portrayed two combatants, clad in elaborate assemblies of sabre fencing helmets, padded leather aprons, cricket leg-pads and heavily padded gloves, sparring with long bamboo staves before an attentive audience.

Quarterstaff play persisted, albeit sporadically, through into the 1880s, becoming particularly associated with the Army's Physical Training Schools at Aldershot Camp and in Madrid, where it was used as a form of training for bayonet fighting (and probably simply enjoyed as a pastime). Photographs show quarterstaff-wielding soldiers clad much as in the Illustrated London News sketch, but also wearing extraordinary sporrans, presumably as a form of groin protection.

In 1883 Sergeant Thomas McCarthy, formerly an instructor of the 7th R.F. and 65th Regiments, published a booklet detailing some of the basic techniques of quarterstaff play, and a set of rules for competitions in that style. Quarterstaff fencing gained a small but loyal following over the subsequent decade, and in 1898 R.G. Allanson-Winn included a chapter on the sport in his book, *Broadsword and Singlestick—with Chapters on Quarter-staff, Bayonet, Cudgel, Shillalah, Walking Stick, Umbrella and other*

Weapons of Self Defence. Notably, neither McCarthy's nor Allanson-Winn's treatments made any reference to specific historical treatises on quarterstaff play. Throughout the 1880s, bouts at quarterstaff were regular features at military exhibitions or "assaults-at-arms."

The original assaults-at-arms in England had been partially inspired by the gymkhana contests undertaken by British soldiers serving in India during the early decades of the 1800s. The word "gymkhana" is actually an Anglo-Hindi portmanteau, from "gym" as in "gymnastic" and "ghend-khana," which means "a place where games are played." Indian cavalrymen traditionally trained in large public arenas, and their feats with lance and sword attracted large, appreciative audiences. By the 1830s the concept had been imported to England as a form of fundraising for military charities, and in June of 1880 British soldiers found themselves charging their horses through an enormous arena in the heart of London, for audiences that sometimes included members of the Royal Family. The Grand Assault-at-Arms, as the largest and most important of these tournaments became known, lost rather a great deal of money for the first several years until the organizers learned to balance competitive events with crowd-pleasing pageantry. Egerton Castle won his gold medal at the Royal Tournament in 1882; within a few years, this grandest of the Grand Assaults had become a well-established fixture in the London sporting and social calendar.

To convey some of the atmosphere and attractions of a typical civilian assault-at-arms during this period, there follows a detailed report on a display at the School of Arms attached to the Inns of Court, which was one of the oldest and most respected legal training centers in England. It was held that lawyers could learn a great deal to their professional advantage by mastering the use of fencing foil and boxing glove.

> "I.C.R.V. ASSAULT-AT-ARMS.
>
> "ON Saturday, May 5, at three o'clock, a large but good-humoured and well-dressed crowd, fortified, it is to be hoped, by a substantial lunch, assembled round the lists, in the I.C.R.V. School of Arms, in Lincoln's-Inn, to exhibit their powers of endurance, in sitting out (as, in the event, they did) a very interesting programme, which lasted, with one interval, from three

o'clock till six. This was the fourth assault-at-arms given by the school, and the whole of the entertainment was provided by its members. A display, including a first-rate exhibition of sword feats and gymnastics was given by a company of gentlemen of the long robe, barristers and students, a large proportion of whom are in actual practice, and the rest of whom are no doubt making vigorous efforts to place themselves in the same category. As to the utility of the school, there is probably no better remedy for the shyness that may paralyse a young man's efforts over his early briefs than the discipline of battle, which will strengthen his fibre, as he stands foil or stick in hand, before some ready master of fence and strives to find an opening for his point, while he is making an opening at the bar. The nice conduct of a small sword is no bad preparation for success, in the fence of tongue, at the bar; and apart from this, fencing, like whist, stands by a man in old age, and its attainment in youth by a town-dweller, will do much to secure him a happy physical old age.

"It would be fastidious for us to give a technical account of the exhibition, for, of course, the events in the programme were displays and not competitions, and it would be invidious to compare the merits of various performers, where each of whom did his best rather to interest the spectators than to conquer an opponent; the only thing, under such circumstances, that can be pronounced upon, is form, and that was thoughout excellent.

"The performance commenced with an excellent display on the parallel bars by Messrs. Jenkin, A. Glen, W. J. Lee, and Mr. T. Gray, Instructor to the School. This was followed by an animated set-to with sticks, between Messrs. J. Reade and C. Phillipps-Wolley; after which, a squad of the I. C. R. V. went through the bayonet-exercise. Boxing, sternest of the arts, was the next attraction, and Mr. R. G. Allanson Winn and Prof. G. Roberts, Instructor to the S. A., made a fine scientific display: after which, an admirable bout of fencing between

Messrs. H. G. Willink and H. A. C. Dunn gave a satisfactory idea of the excellence, in this difficult mystery, of the members of the School. Both fenced in correct form, and with evident intelligence.

"Now came a great feature: Mr. Hugh Pollock's sword feats. As a rule, at an assault-at-arms, the sword feats have to be left out, or rare professional talent has to be imported. Mr. Pollock's performance included cutting the feather, which we do not remember ever seeing attempted by anyone, in the face of the people, but in which the swordsman was successful at his first attempt; and the very unusual variation of cutting lead, with the left as well as the right—a feat which Richard the lion-hearted might have shrunk from attempting; and the cut through the threaded potato, which would very likely have taken up a great deal of Saladin's valuable time in the learning.

"Interesting boxing ensued, between Mr. F. E. Speed and Corporal Major Storror, Instructor to the S. A.

"The play at Quarter Staff, between Messrs. P. Payne and J. Reade, was very popular, and evoked something of the unforced merriment to be met with among the juvenile element at a Punch and Judy show, when the Hero of that great drama goes into action with one of his numerous antagonists.

"The remaining numbers of this part of the programme consisted of Bayonet v. Bayonet, between Messrs. W. Brinton and Allanson Winn, and the lance exercise, by Messrs. H. Pollock, Reade, T. F. Hobson and R. F. Norton. After an interval, during which a general melee took place among the gentlemen in order to obtain tea and coffee for the ladies, the horizontal bar was placed in position; the same gymnastic team as before delighted the audience with a first-class display; then came some capital boxing between Mr. R. C. Lehtnann and Professor G. Roberts. A graceful display of Indian clubs was then given by a team consisting of Messrs. Brinton, Reade, Lee, and A. Cane, under the leadership of Mr. Jenkin, at the conclusion of which Mr. Jenkin gave a still more intricate exhibition of

> clubs, which was much admired. Next the audience welcomed Mr. F. Pollock and Instructor Blackburn, in a battle with the foils; Mr. F. Pollock, bearing himself with great spirit against the master who was opposed to him. This was a fine display. Upon this followed a rattling encounter with sticks between Messrs. R. H. Simonds and Payne.
>
> "The spectators were next entertained with three good substantial rounds of boxing, between Mr. Wolley and Corporal-Major Storror, and then the vaulting horse, with a terrifying game of leap-frog in mid-air, on the high horse, by the same gymnastic team, with the addition of Mr. H. Brushfield. The other items of the programme, consisting in a sword v. bayonet tussle between Messrs. Simonds and Bunton, and the cavalry sword exercise, which was brilliantly performed by a team composed of Messrs. H. Pollock, Reade, Hobson, and Brushfield. Captain G. Drinkwater was master of the lists.
>
> "As to the general interest of the show, we will only say this: that we have never had a better ten-shillings-worth for a shilling before, and do not expect to again—until next year."
>
> – *Pump Court: the Temple newspaper and review*, Volume 7, 1888

Unsurprisingly, it is also in the context of the assault-at-arms that we first encounter revivals of sword and dagger fencing in England. As early as 1869, newspaper reports on "grand assaults" began to refer to "ancient combats." These competitive bouts, in which fencers were armed with pairs of foils, or a foil and a dagger each, were evidently in conscious imitation of historical sword and dagger fencing.

> "The next item on the programme was an ancient combat between Sergeant-Major Steel and Sergeant Adams ... the novelty being that the fencing was carried on with four foils instead of two, but although the performers made several good hits, and exhibited a considerable amount of dexterity and

tact, we could not help thinking that the exercise was a somewhat ridiculous one, in the face of the many improvements of modern times."

– *Hampshire Telegraph and Sussex Chronicle*, October 9, 1869

"Instructor O'Neal and Instructor Pillinger afforded a sample of what was termed an 'ancient combat.' Both parties were armed with a sword in the right hand and a dirk in the left, and made a furious assault on one another."

– *Belfast News*, April 28, 1873

Similar double-weapon bouts, consistently described as "ancient combats" in newspaper notices and programme notes, were held at assault-at-arms exhibitions throughout this period. An entrepreneur named Mr. Stodare even commercialized the style in 1880, advertising rapier and dagger fencing among a wide range of martial displays available for fetes and galas during the summer season.

Unfortunately, again, these references omit crucial details, particularly as to whether these "ancient combats" were actually reconstructions of any specific historical system, or were simply inspired, in a general sense, by the play of the sword and dagger. It is also possible that they were inspired by the reconstructions of Villaamil and his coterie of antiquarian fencers in Madrid. Even if this form of swordplay was largely improvised, however, it seems to have frequently been performed with considerable verve and skill:

"Corporal-Major Newton, 1st Life Guards, and Corporal Dickson, of the same regiment, displayed a dexterity that blood-thirsty swashbucklers of the Cavalier period might have envied. In parrying with the dagger Newton especially was very quick. Again and again he allowed the point of his opponent's foil almost to touch his breast, when with the shorter blade he right deftly returned the blow."

– *Daily News*, August 30, 1883

It is evident that the practice of reviving historical styles of fencing was present in Europe from the 1850s onwards, in at least three modes. Villaamil and his associates appear to have been part of a project to re-invigorate an elderly, but still living tradition of Spanish swordsmanship via an infusion of theories and practices drawn from an earlier incarnation of that same tradition, as recorded by de Rada. The quarterstaff revival associated with the Aldershot military school is not known to have drawn directly from any established historical source, but was more in the nature of a recreational fencing sport inspired by the generic tradition of fighting with two-handed staves. Lacking specific evidence to the contrary, much the same can be surmised of the sword-and-dagger combats associated with Assaults-at-Arms during the 1870s.

Although seemingly sporadic and scattered, the groundwork was in place for a systematic and wide-ranging revival of ancient swordplay. It remained for Hutton and Castle to take up that gauntlet.

Hutton and Castle perform an exhibition at arms for the Prince of Wales (March 20, 1891).

Chapter 5:

The First Generation

German-born Dorette Wilke immigrated to England as a young teenager in 1885. Wilke later reported that, having enrolled in Adolf A. Stempel's gymnasium in Albany Park, she studied both classical French foil fencing with French masters, and also the fencing of the 16th century, being tutored by none other than Alfred Hutton. Wilke went on to become a famous and influential teacher of physical culture in her own right. If her recollection was correct, then she may have been among the first students of Hutton's ancient swordplay.

Intriguingly, Hutton dedicated his book *Sword and the Centuries: or, Old Sword Days and Old Sword Ways* (1901), to "my bright brave-hearted little child-friend and pupil, Charlie Sefton." This is a reference to the child actor Charles Sefton, who had starred as Arthur in Beerbohm Tree's production of *King John* in 1899. Captain Hutton was in great demand as a theatrical fight choreographer at that time, so it is likely that Sefton had become his student in that connection. Later, in chapter IX ("The Rapier and its Auxiliaries"), Hutton again referred to Sefton:

> "When the cloak took, as it occasionally did, the place of the dagger, it was rolled twice round the left arm, and the thrusts were dashed aside by the pendant folds, and it was sometimes thrown in various ways in such a manner as to completely

envelop the person, or so to entangle the sword of the enemy that he was for the moment entirely at the mercy of the thrower. This fight was very easy to acquire, and Swetnam says that in a very few lessons a boy of fifteen can learn to defend himself against any man whatsoever; and indeed, we ourselves know a little boy of that age, Master Charles Sefton, who more than holds his own with the gentleman who has taught him (i.e., Hutton himself)."

In the Introduction to *Sword and the Centuries,* Hutton further reminisced about young soldiers and schoolboys learning historical fencing at the School of Arms of the London Rifle Brigade. Prominent among them was Cyril Matthey, a member of the L.R.B. who had started fencing in 1876, at the age of twelve. Eight years later, Matthey was the chief instructor of the L.R.B. School of Arms. His students included eleven-year old Ernest Stenson Cooke, Frank Herbert Whittow (aged around twelve at the time), and the teenage E.D. Johnson and W.P. Gate. It is likely that Egerton Castle might have occasionally taken some active part in the L.R.B. classes as well.

It seems that these classes were not part of the official physical culture program offered to L.R.B. soldiers, but were something more in the nature of an extra-curricular activity—a "boys' club" centered upon the revival of ancient swordplay. Hutton described their historical fencing tutor as "an enthusiastic student of old arms and old fighting," which is undoubtedly a modest reference to himself. As they gained in years and experience, the eager young students would then go out and perform their own demonstrations of ancient fencing at local secondary schools.

At Bradfield College, Hutton noted, his students' presentation had been met with such enthusiasm that the following year, the Bradfield boys reciprocated with their own demonstration of historical fencing skills, in a performance staged in the College's Greek Theatre. Built in 1888 and still in active use today, this outdoor theatre hosted a unique presentation of fight scenes from the plays of William Shakespeare, in which the weapons used were all of the Elizabethan period. Given the inspiration offered by the L.R.B. School of Arms students, this school play may have been among the first English stage productions to have been directly influenced by Hutton's historical fencing research. As we shall see, there would be many more in the years to come.

Along with Hutton and Castle themselves, this core group of young men—Matthey, Whittow, Stenson Cooke, Johnson and Gate—would go on to form the nucleus of the ancient swordplay revival in England.

Captain Hutton and Dr. Mount-Biggs demonstrate sword and buckler fencing for the Prince of Wales

Chapter 6

Exhibitions of Ancient Swordplay (1888–92)

By the last decade of the 1800s, ancient swordplay had gained enough momentum to no longer be a novelty—at least to the informed public. This is one of the reasons why, during this period, we have evidence of several presentations, possibly inspired by Castle's *Schools and Masters of Fence,*" that sought to infuse the traditional assault-at-arms with various historically-inspired forms of swordplay. And this evidence gives us the chance to get acquainted with other interesting *dramatis personae* of this revivalist movement.

In early 1888, Austrian Fechtmeister (fencing master) Johann Hartl organized an unusual travelling fencing display. According to his press releases, Hartl had specialized in training young Viennese society women in various fencing skills, and had persuaded their parents to allow him to escort their daughters on a vaudeville and music hall tour through Europe and the USA, exhibiting their skills with "rapiers" (actually foils) and daggers, cavalry sabres and two-handed swords. They also demonstrated gladiatorial combats with the net and trident. For some time, the troupe was based at the Eden Musee, a vaudeville house in New York City, and they toured widely throughout the country, including engagements in Boston and Chicago. In August of 1888, the Hartl troupe suffered a setback when they found themselves stranded in Boston due to a disagreement with a local promoter. Newspaper reports noted that they made their way back to New York "as best as they could," and that they were considering suing the promoter for breach of contract.

The Hartl troupe's performances actually sparked a brief craze for foil and dagger fencing among well-to-do American women, and fencing bibliophile Carl Thimm recorded a positive review of one of their performances in London.

On June 29th, 1889, a demonstration of rapier and dagger fencing based on Vincentio Saviolo's system was performed at a "Medieval Tournament" in Montreal, Canada.

This event was directed by David Legault, who had established the Guards of the Archiepiscopal Palace and who was also the founder of a successful physical culture school, where he taught fencing as well as Greco-Roman wrestling and gymnastics. The rapier and dagger exhibition at the Montreal tournament was performed by L.J. Chartrand, a provost at Legault's academy, and by a Lieutenant Mallette. Also on display at the tournament was a curious form of elevated jousting, in which two men standing upon raised platforms "fenced" with what appear to have been jousting lances while defending themselves with kite shields.

It is clear that, during this period, most exhibitions of historical fencing were undertaken for amusement, commercial gain, or both. In many cases, the only surviving records are newspaper reports that do not offer enough detail for us to be able to judge the degree of historical accuracy that may have been attempted by the performers, although there seems no doubt that the exhibitions by the L.R.B.'s School of Arms club, and those by Castle, et al at the Kernoozers Club, would have been among the most highly accurate for their time.

It was also in 1889 that Egerton Castle first tried his hand at theatrical fight choreography. Assisted by Walter Pollock, he staged the fight sequences for Richard Mansfield's production of *Richard III* at the Globe Theatre with, we may be assured, more than the usual level of concern for historical accuracy.

Castle had also been hard at work on his first novel, *Consequences*, which was published in early 1891. Perhaps inspired by the trend towards practical exhibitions of historical fencing, he then initiated what may have been his first formal, public collaboration with Captain Hutton, described here in a contemporary newspaper review entitled, as was the exhibition itself, *The Story of Swordsmanship*:

> "Some fourteen years ago Mr. Egerton Castle was so impressed with the admirable fencing of Mr. Irving as Hamlet, that the spectator determined to acquire the art himself. Not only has Mr. Castle become one of its most skilful exponents, but he has devoted much time and research to its history, and the result was given us on Wednesday afternoon, Feb. 25th, on the stage of the Lyceum (kindly lent by Mr. Irving). We heard a most interesting paper read by Mr. Castle, entitled *The Story of Swordsmanship, specially considered in connection with the Rise and Decline of Duelling.* Would that there were space available to enlarge on the merits of the discourse, for, considering its limits, it was most comprehensive, and quoted the best authorities on the subject! The various weapons in the shape of swords, daggers, rapiers, and foils, and their special uses, were illustrated in the most finished and masterly manner by Mr. Egerton Castle, Captain A. Hutton, Dr. Mount-Biggs, Sir Frederick and Mr. Walter Pollock, Professor Vital de Bailly (sic), and Maitre-d'armes Philippe Bourgeois, all good men and true, the two latter specially well versed in l'escrime."
>
> – *Dramatic Notes*, Volumes 12–13, 1891

A reviewer from *The Stage* offered a glowing report on the Lyceum Theatre presentation, also offering the detail that "Mr. Castle's wrist is stronger than his voice, and we are fain to confess that some portions of his delivery were inaudible to us." The audience of three hundred guests were seated on bleachers on the giant stage of the Lyceum, with their backs to the orchestra pit; an arrangement that conjured an ambience closer to that of a lecture hall than of a traditional theatrical presentation.

The Journal of the Society of Antiquaries offered this review:

"One of the curious revivals of intelligent interest in the customs and practices of the past received a decided impetus last month on the stage of the Lyceum, at the hands of an able antiquary. Mr. Irving, himself an expert in the art of fencing, placed his stage at the disposal of Mr. Egerton Castle, F.S.A., for an afternoon lecture on *The History of Swordsmanship*, with practical illustrations by the lecturer and his brother swordsmen of the theory and method of the duello. Mr. Egerton Castle, well known as the author of *Masters of Fence*, traced with much circumstance the origin of single combat as the outcome of obsolete jousts and tournaments. The judicial acceptance of trial by combat brought about the study of systematic fencing. The old wagers of battle with great heavy two-handed swords were illustrated by an encounter with these weapons between the lecturer and Captain Hutton, the author of *Cold Steel*. To this succeeded a bout between Captain Hutton and Dr. Mount-Biggs that brought vividly before the audience that once prevalent and national 'pastime' of sword and buckler. But soon the sturdy English broadsword made way for the elegant and more deadly rapier—a foreign exotic—with its artificial and yet graceful rules of deportment. The systematic fencing of the Early Italian school, carefully described and illustrated, was followed by the most interesting part of this vivid lecture, that dealt with cavalier fencing of the Elizabethan time. The lecturer sustained the character of the great master, Vincentio, and Mr. Walter Pollock that of his pupil, Luke. A further illustration of the duello of that period was a rapier and dagger bout between the same gentlemen.

"Another remarkable combat was that between Mr. Egerton Castle with sword and cloak, against Sir Frederick Pollock with sword and dagger. To this succeeded, in rapid succession, descriptions, both by word of mouth and

> strength of wrist, of English backsword play, of the nimble small-sword practice of the eighteenth century, and of foil play both of the French and Italian schools. On the stage was grouped a brilliant and historic display of old examples of the weapons of the duello, lent by our contributor, the Baron de Cosson, F.S.A., and by other members of the Kernoozers Club. Mr. Egerton Castle is to be heartily congratulated on the entire success of this happily-conceived and admirably-executed 'lecture.'"
>
> – *The Antiquary,* Volume 23, 1891

A *Daily News* journalist was taken by some of Castle's more arcane tales of historical masters including Achille Marozzo and Camillo Agrippa:

> "It is curious to think that some of these pedantic fencing masters professed to be in possession of the secret of a universal parry and an unescapable thrust. But theirs was the age of the philosopher's stone and the universal solvent …
>
> "A whimsically complex diagram of fencing—that invented by Girard Thibault, of Antwerp—was next exhibited. "Rubbish," Mr. Castle called it, and yet poor old Girard worried his soul over it all his life long, and put the results into a Brobdingnagian book (also exhibited) that almost required a wheelbarrow to carry it off."
>
> – *Daily News,* February 26, 1891.

Additional reports suggest that a giant facsimile of Thibault's famous diagram had actually been "flown" onto the Lyceum stage with wires, like a theatrical backdrop. It is evident that Egerton Castle was bemused by the esoteric geometries and theorems of Thibault's system of fence. Ironically, Thibault's method was a branch of la Verdadera Destreza; the same school that had itself been subject to a systematic revival in Madrid, some thirty years earlier. Recent scholarship suggests that this method is rather more effective than the young Castle may have credited.

A reviewer from *the Speaker* picked up on another of Castle's lecture themes, which, as we shall see, was also a concern of Captain Hutton's; namely, the symbolism and function of the duel of honor. Whereas dueling per se had been not only illegal, but also very deeply unfashionable in England for many decades, it still occurred in some countries on the European continent. The reviewer noted that:

> "Most English people have made up their minds that the duel is pure barbarism, conceived in folly and executed in bloodthirstiness, admitting of no defence. Probably they are right, but *de omnibus dubitandum est,* and one wonders if their conviction is never assailed by the least doubt. Is it quite certain that if a man's honour were grossly affronted to-day, and in a manner for which the law either could not or would not give him technical redress, and if he were to provoke the offender to a duel and run him through the body, there would not be a strong current of popular feeling in his favour? Or perhaps we should rather say, that a considerable weft of sympathy and excuse would not run across the warp of censure?
>
> "The duel has, of course, the tendency in one direction to create the swash-buckler—the man who is always ready to 'get into difficulties by word of mouth, and out of them by deed of point.' But has it no tendency to maintain a standard of at least formal courtesy, and is it not a fact that the liability to be suddenly called upon to take one's life in one's hand has an elevating and sobering effect upon the character? As for manners, consider the two phases of modern society where a personal affront leads inevitably to a hostile encounter—those of the fighting German student and the cowboy—the real cowboy, of course, not the drunken rowdy of the frontier bar. After making the proper local allowances, is it quite clear that the standard of manners there is lower than that of the Strand or the Underground Railway? Civilisation is an ideal

goal, but is there no danger, as Mr. Egerton Castle—who, by the way, had not a word of defence for the serious practice of his art—remarked, of being "civilised out of all manhood"?

"And it is curious, in conclusion, to reflect that the growth of the independence of woman is coincident with the decline of duelling, whatever may be cause or effect. From the days of Tubal Cain to that when Peg Woffington pinned her roses on Angelo's breast, nine duels out of ten have been fought because of a woman. But it is impossible to fight for a woman who is capable and desirous of taking care of herself. No doubt, it is best that she should, and therefore one's feeling on the subject is probably only a natural and praiseworthy wonder as to just what are the new virtues coming to replace the courage and the charm that constituted the ideal relation of men and women in the days when the sword and society were in vital connection."

– "The Sword and Society," *The Speaker,* February 28, 1891

It is noteworthy that reviews of the Lyceum theatre exhibition further confirm that Sir Frederick Pollock, as well as his younger brother Walter, were actively involved in "ancient swordplay" during this period. Of course, Sir Frederick's essay and lecture on fencing history had been among Castle's motivations to write *Schools and Masters of Fence* seven years earlier, and all three men were active members of the Kernoozers Club. In that connection, journalist M.H. Spielmann, who had witnessed one of the Club's private ancient swordplay exhibitions, described Sir Frederick's fencing as being "more temperamental than academical"

Other than completing the circle begun in 1883, when the young Egerton Castle had been inspired by Henry Irving's stage fencing, the Lyceum Theatre exhibition was highly significant in that it was the first time that the experiments of Hutton and Castle had been presented for public approval. The event was also very widely and positively reviewed in well-regarded newspapers.

It's important to underscore that many of these men were wealthy, professionally distinguished and socially influential in the extremely class-conscious London of the 1890s. Such a demonstration, hosted by the famous Henry Irving and attended by numerous political, sporting and military notables, would perhaps be roughly equivalent to a martial arts exhibition presented by Sir Ian McKellen and featuring demonstrations by Jackie Chan, retired Mixed Martial Arts champion Frank Shamrock and a member of the U.S. Supreme Court judiciary. Little wonder that the event briefly became the talk of London society, especially when Edward VII, the Prince of Wales, wrote to Mr. Irving and asked if the display might be repeated so that he and his friends could see it. Of course, the display was duly repeated for the Prince and his entourage, the return engagement taking place on March 20th of 1891.

Three months later, Cyril Matthey fenced with C.E.F. Mount-Biggs at swords and bucklers, and Captain Hutton challenged Walter Pollock at rapiers and daggers, in a display appended to a production of a 17th-century play, *The Masque of Flowers*. Staged in the Inner Temple-Hall, all proceeds went to St. Michael's Convalescent Home in Westgate-on-Sea, establishing a charitable precedent that was to be followed many times over the next decade.

In November of the same year, Sir Frederick Pollock delivered a lecture on *The History of the Sword* for his colleagues at the Inns of Court, illustrated by practical demonstrations performed by his younger brother Walter, Egerton Castle, H.A. Dunn and a Mr. Blackburn.

It was also in 1891 that Hutton's associate and sometime student in historical fencing, Carl Thimm, published his *Complete Bibliography of the Art of Fence*. This was a comprehensive catalogue of books on fencing and all manner of related subjects including some that were, according to Castle, so tangentially related as to be basically irrelevant. The book was, however, generally well-received:

> "Mr. Carl A. Thimm's *Complete Bibliography of Fencing and Duelling practised by all European Nations from the Middle Ages to the Present Day* is an elaborate, handsomely equipped work, that betokens much painstaking research on the part of its author. In England the art and practice of fencing, long

seemingly moribund, seems to have shown of late years unmistakable signs of revival. This revival, bringing with it an interest in the rather copious and generally unfamiliar literature of the subject, has created a need for a work like the present one—that is, for a systematic and fairly exhaustive guide or index to that literature. Whether or not such a guide is needed in this country, we do not undertake to say; but we have no doubt at all that Mr. Thimm's is by far the best one obtainable.

"Mr. Thimm is not without predecessors in his somewhat curious line of research—such men as Pallavicini in the seventeenth century, Kahn in the eighteenth, Roux and Possellier in the earlier part of the present one, having published bibliographies of works touching the swordsman's art; but these books contained at best but snippets of information on a very wide subject. Mr. Thimm's immediate predecessor is M. Vigeant, the Parisian maître d'armes and littérateur, author of an elegant little book entitled *La Bibliographie de l'Escrime, Ancienne et Moderne*. M. Vigeant's is a trustworthy account of French works, but it cannot compete with that of Mr. Thimm in point of general completeness. The latter bibliography is intended as a work of reference for all interested in fencing and duelling, bayonet exercise, etc., the author having accepted the definition that the subject of fence embraces 'all works relating to the art of offence and defence with all weapons held in the hands'—that is, of all non-ballistic or non-projectile weapons, from foil to bayonet, and from dagger to battle-axe. The volume also enumerates all books and manuscripts relating to duelling, together with newspaper and magazine articles in print that have fallen under the author's observation. The volume is of considerable pictorial and quasi-pictorial interest, as it contains facsimile reproductions of rare title-pages, frontispieces, portraits of certain leading experts and masters ancient and modern, etc. There is also a well-executed portrait of the compiler."

– *The Dial*, Volumes 22–23, 1897

With this work, the corpus of 19th-century scholarly efforts on historical swordsmanship became nothing short of monumental. But while this kept catalyzing interest in academic and research circles, how (if at all) did it spill over into the practical side of combat? The last decades of the Victorian era saw many conflicts in the far corners of the British empire, many of which were against indigenous warriors armed with bladed weapons (e.g., the Zulus in 1879). Surely, to the minds of proponents of ancient swordplay, the rifle-bayonet, the lance and the sabre could have used an infusion of fresh techniques from the old treatises. This idea was pursued by some, most notably the indefatigable Alfred Hutton, who embarked upon a crusade with the goal of influencing military training with the principles and actions of ancient swordsmanship.

John Ernest Breun's portrait of Captain Hutton, entitled *Cold Steel* and reproduced in the Captain's book of that name, won the gold medal in a competition held at the Paris Salon in 1892. The success of both book and portrait quickly earned Hutton the nickname of "Cold Steel" among his friends.

Chapter 7

Hutton's *Cold Steel* and *Old Sword Play*

Alfred Hutton, just as much as his friend Egerton Castle, was devoted to the art of the sword in all of its forms, and in one area in particular his interest evidently exceeded Castle's. As well as reviving historical systems out of antiquarian interest, Hutton had continued to publish books on military close-combat with weapons, including *Swordsmanship, for the use of Soldiers* (1887), *Cold Steel* and *Fixed Bayonets: A Complete System of Fence for the British Magazine Rifle* (both in 1890). Captain Hutton held a deep and long-standing concern about the standard of training in close-combat skills being offered to British soldiers, particularly in the wake of numerous reports that they were coming off second-best in hand-to-hand skirmishes against Zulu, Afridi and Maori warriors and other indigenous peoples throughout the Empire. Hutton's role in the controversy surrounding military close-combat training is examined in chapters eight and nine.

Part of the aim of the Royal Tournament and Assault at Arms, in which Egerton Castle had competed so successfully a few years previously, was to encourage soldiers and officers to develop greater skill in combat with the sabre, bayonet, lance and other weapons. However, Captain Hutton recognized the drawbacks, as well as the advantages, created by the artificial conventions of sporting competition. The system of military sabre fencing proposed in *Cold Steel*, for example, was largely based on a combination of the systems of Domenico Angelo, the then-contemporary Italian school of sabre fence and the works of various 18th-century backsword masters, but it also referenced several much earlier works. Hutton was attempting to devise a system of practical fighting with the English cavalry sabre, as distinct from either duelling or academic school play, which had become the basis for military instruction. Further chapters in *Cold Steel* addressed the use of the dagger and unarmed defence against the dagger (after Marozzo), military sabre vs. rifle-bayonet, the policeman's truncheon, and similar methods that might be used in practical, real-world fighting. His efforts to revive antique forms of close-combat met with some skepticism in military circles:

> "Among the latter are '14 seizures, after Achille Marozzo, 1536.' These represent various modes of defence by an unarmed man against one armed with a dagger. The armed man must be very unready or very stupid to allow himself to be mastered so easily."
>
> – *The United Service Magazine*, Volume 73, 1889

Such criticism aside, this personal goal of Hutton's was to manifest itself in much of his writing, and increasingly also in his lectures and demonstrations, as we shall see.

It was in 1892 that Hutton published his first practical treatment specifically devoted to ancient styles of fence. *Old Sword Play* was an illustrated survey of fencing systems of the 16th, 17th, and 18th centuries, including 58 pictures from Alfieri, Angelo, Di Grassi, Liancourt, Marozzo and other famous masters. Used as an instructional manual, this book might be used to perform some of the plays of the two-handed sword, rapier and dagger, rapier and cloak, dagger and cloak, broadsword and buckler, case of rapiers and the smallsword.

Old Sword Play was well-received by the critics:

> "Captain Hutton has compiled and arranged the lessons in his book so as to make the antique methods accessible to the student without the labour of searching through many ancient volumes."
>
> – *Graphic.*

"Captain Hutton's clear and concise treatment of this curious form of Sword Play, illustrated as it is by plates from Marozzo and Di Grassi, is extremely interesting. This latest contribution to the literature of fencing should not be neglected by anyone interested in that fine art."

– *Illustrated London News.*

"The plates are superbly reproduced, and form a most valuable collection."

– *Saturday Review.*

In his preface, Hutton noted that:

"There are those who affect to ridicule the study of obsolete weapons, alleging that it is of no practical use; everything, however, is useful to the Art of Fence which tends to create an interest in it, and certain it is that such contests as 'Rapier and Dagger,' 'Two Hand Sword,' or 'Broadsword and Handbuckler,' are a very great embellishment to the somewhat monotonous proceedings of the ordinary 'assault of arms.'"

In fact, it is evident that *Old Swordplay* was not an attempt to present historical fencing styles per se. The book reads rather as if it had originated as an in-house manual for the members of the L.R.B. School of Arms, being released to the public when the study of ancient swordplay was attracting a degree of mainstream attention. If this is so, then it is an example of Alfred Hutton having "re-purposed" techniques from an eclectic range of historical sources towards his own ends.

Despite the presence of, for example, numerous cutting techniques in historically earlier systems of rapier play, and of thrusts in antagonistic sword and buckler fencing, Hutton's chapter on rapier fencing includes only thrusting techniques and his section on sword and buckler omits thrusts. These omissions would make little sense if his object was to present a particular historical style verbatim. However, they do make some sense if they are taken to represent artificial conventions for the purpose of bouting, and most particularly, of bouting for the purposes of public display, with the object of demonstrating historically generic, as opposed to treatise-specific, fencing systems to an audience of interested laypeople.

In introducing the rapier and dagger, Hutton commented:

> "In early times the edges were undoubtedly used, but they were by degrees abandoned in favour of the swifter and more deadly point. In our revival of this practice, therefore, we shall adhere to pure point-play, and we shall reserve that of the edge for the sword and buckler, in which it plays the most important part."

Similarly, in a 1902 speech for the London Playgoer's Club, Hutton was to note that, "in our revived rapier play, we make use of the point only."

In discussing sword and buckler fencing via Achille Marozzo's *Opera Nova* (1536) Hutton twice refers to de-emphasizing or eliminating the use of the point. Reports on the L.R.B. group's exhibitions of sword and buckler fencing consistently refer to the fury of their cutting attacks but, conspicuously, make no reference to thrusts. Both Hutton's lectures and published reviews of the L.R.B. School of Arms' bouting displays suggest that their sword and buckler fencing usually represented the agonistic, sporting play of Elizabethan bravos, rather than the more earnest fence of those weapons in actual, life-or-death combat. Emphasizing cuts to the exclusion of thrusts in sword and buckler play would also serve as a useful point of contrast between exhibitions of that system and of rapier fencing.

By the same token, safety in bouting must have been a mitigating factor with regards to historical accuracy. Hutton noted that "the true edge cuts 3 and 4, at or below the knee, we do not permit, on account of the danger of inflicting serious injury." This is somewhat curious in that quarterstaff and singlestick fencers made effective use of cricket leg pads in safeguarding against strikes to the knees and shins. Perhaps Hutton's group objected to cricket pads on esthetic grounds.

The final chapters deal largely with various methods of closing with and disarming an adversary in rapier and smallsword play, representing another of Hutton's special interests. Descriptions of his theatrical fight choreography frequently refer to the use of grappling and disarming techniques, which were distinct enough from the theatrical norms of the time to warrant special mention.

Thus, the suggestion is that in selecting material for *Old Sword Play,* Hutton methodically chose those historical techniques (and illustrations) that best supported his group's approach to free-bouting at assaults-at-arms and in performing set-plays, either for educational display or for theatrical fight choreography. Stage combat was yet another of Hutton's interests in the application of his art, and one that was very much shared by Egerton Castle as well. It is also significant that Hutton highlighted the utility of presentations of ancient swordplay as a means of attracting attention to the modern sport of competitive fencing.

The following year, Castle collaborated with Walter Pollock on writing a play entitled *Saviolo,* a fanciful tale based on the character of Elizabethan-era fencing master Vincentio Saviolo, which was written for Henry Irving. Irving bought an option on the play, but did not actually stage it at the Lyceum. However, as we shall see, Castle was to return to *Saviolo,* in various shapes and guises, throughout his literary and theatrical careers.

An Elizabethan duel, under the direction of Captain Hutton, performed at the Hippodrome – *The Graphic* (July 19, 1902).

Chapter 8

Verie Many Weapons: More Exhibitions of Ancient Swordplay (1893–6)

During January of 1893, Hutton delivered a lecture and demonstration on *Swordplay, Ancient and Modern* at Toynbee Hall, and the following month, both Hutton and Castle were involved in another elaborate assault-at-arms display. This one took place at Oxford University on February 23rd, and was in support of the newly founded Oxford Fencing Club. The exhibition was a spectacular affair, divided into three sections, each introduced by a selection of appropriate music performed by a small orchestra.

The first section showcased a series of bouts with the foil and epée and the second began with a "brief allocution by the (Fencing Club) President Sir Frederick Pollock, explaining the transition of swordsmanship from the old English Sword and Buckler fight to Rapier and Dagger," illustrated by a re-creation of an "Elizabethan prize at verie many weapons" (rapier and dagger, sword and buckler, and sword and cloak). The third section featured bouts of foil, sabre, and epée fencing, a mixed-styles contest of epée versus sabre, and the assault-at-arms concluded with a display of Highland broadsword and target fencing.

A commemorative sketch of this event portrays Hutton and Castle engaged at rapier and dagger versus sword and buckler; the buckler-man is wearing an elaborate sporran, very reminiscent of those worn by quarterstaff fencers at Aldershot camp.

The following month, Hutton, Castle, Stenson Cooke, Gate and Harvest were the principals in an assault-at-arms and charitable fund-raiser in aid of providing a headquarters and club for the boys of the First Cade Battalion of the Queen's (First Surrey). The rapier and cloak match between young Stenson Cooke and Gate garnered particularly warm applause.

Hutton followed this demonstration with a lecture entitled *Our Swordsmanship,* delivered for an audience at Royal United Service Institution, Whitehall. In this presentation he developed his criticism of the state of military swordplay in the British Army, asserting that "the want of enthusiasm for swordsmanship is largely due to the apathy of the governing bodies and headmasters of our great schools," who, Hutton said, typically did not offer fencing at all in their "Army classes." He also spoke disparagingly of the missed opportunities of fencing instruction at Aldershot Camp, which, he claimed, were due to young officers being disinclined to train because of poor instruction and a lack of proper facilities. He was careful not to apportion blame to the instructors themselves, but rather to their being compelled to teach a "clumsy" system of fencing that they knew did not actually work. Hutton took pains to point out that, if the officials at Aldershot had availed themselves of the services of professional fencing masters when the training camp had first been established some thirty years earlier, it might have developed a fencing school to rival that of the famous, and much admired, Joinville Military Academy in France.

In May, Hutton participated in another exhibition of ancient swordplay, this time under the auspices of the King's Dragoon Guards commanded by Lieutenant-Colonel Douglas Willan. The display was held at the Windsor Cavalry Barracks and was attended by notables including Prince and Princess Henry of Battenberg, General Lord Methuen, Major-General Sir John and Lady Cowell, General Sayer, General Marter and Colonel Yermaloff of the Russian Military Attache. The theme was to compare historical with modern forms of fencing.

A stage, similar to those used in prize-fighting, was erected upon the lawn, the audience was seated about it in rows, with soldiers watching from the balconies of their barracks. The regimental band of the King's Dragoons played suitably stirring music up until the first of the combats was about to commence, and then carefully laid their instruments down on the grass and prepared to watch their officers "have at" each other.

A detailed report offered by a reviewer from the Pall Mall Gazette offers some insight into both the mood and the practical specifics of the Windsor display. It was announced that the umpire would not declare the winners, so that the audience could judge the outcome of each bout for themselves.

The display commenced with a bout at broadsword and buckler between Lieutenants Marter and Deacon.

> "When the word was given yesterday the combatants began prancing about the stage like two North American Indians on the war path looking for a tomahawk opening. Their knees were bent, their bodies were bent, and only their necks were upright, as they bounded from side to side, making cuts that fell upon the bucklers, and made them ring. Within thirty seconds of the start one of the combatants would have had a gash a foot deep in his left side, had the battle been for blood."
>
> – *Pall Mall Gazette*, May 2 1893

The next contest was at rapiers and daggers between Mr. H. F. Langton, substituting for Mr. F.H. Fernie who was unable to compete due to injury, and a Mr. Hulton:

> "While they fought, the first rank of ladies were busily engaged in discussing the size of Julia Nelson's hats and wondering how she kept them on. Both combatants being impervious, on account of their leather jackets and the buttons on swords and daggers, each was able to bow to two out of the four points of the compass and then walk off the stage."
>
> – Ibid.

In the next bout, Captain Hutton was adjudged by the Pall Mall Gazette reviewer to have lost at foils against Major R.C.B. Lawrence. Then H. de. C. Eastwood and Mr. Langton contested with rapiers and cloaks:

> "The cloak is worn over the left arm as a buckler. It is proper to throw it at your antagonist if by doing so you can sufficiently disconcert him to plant your rapier in some yielding part of his person. Still, this is a risky trick, for if he dodges the cloak you are left without a buckler. Mr. Langton grabbed his opponent's cloak at one stage of the game, and then gave him several imaginary inches of cold steel in a most business-like way. Once you get your man on the run in the rapier-and-cloak game, you can fill his back with holes."
>
> – Ibid.

The following display was by Captain Hutton and Sergeant-Instructor Walker, and consisted of a "set-play" demonstration of two-handed swords, it being explained to the audience that the swords were too heavy, and therefore the strikes and thrusts too dangerous, to be used in free bouting:

> "So they went at it, one-two, one-two-three-four, and then rested. When the swords met they rang loud and clear. Both combatants took their time, neither evinced the slightest desire to make a pass at the other without giving warning of his intention. If they weren't less polite in the sixteenth century, two handed sword play must have been slow enough for a funeral."
>
> – Ibid.

Major Lawrence and Sergeant-Instructor Walker then fought an epee "duel," and then Captain T. Bogle-Smith, armed with rapier and dagger, engaged with Mr. Eastwood, who used the sword and buckler:

> "For some time the combat was even, but pulling himself together at the last call of 'time!', Mr. Eastwood ran in on his man, and, paying attention to two prods in the diaphragm, fell upon Captain Bogle-Smith and smote him twice across the nape of the neck, to the great delight of the spectators, the private soldiers going into convulsions in the most open way."
>
> – Ibid.

There followed a set-play demonstration with the smallsword between Major Lawrence and Mr. Eastwood, which borrowed heavily from De Liancour's treatise of 1686 and was described by the reviewer as being "not sufficiently rapid to be interesting." Next was a bout at sabres and then a cloak and dagger combat between Mr. J. A Berners and Mr. F. Deacon, which was well-received by the audience:

> "The game requires extreme agility, and both combatants possessed this in a most satisfactory degree. They bounded over the stage as if they were seven-eighths gutta-percha (rubber – Ed.) and jabbed at each other in the most reckless way, the spectators applauding vigourously at the earnestness of the players."
>
> – Ibid.

Major Lawrence and Mr. Bell-Smith then fenced, each armed with a case of rapiers, i.e., a sword in each hand. The grand finale was a four-man rapier and dagger duel between Captain Bogle-Smith (seconded by Mr. Eastwood) and Captain W.J.S. Ferguson (seconded by Mr. Hulton.):

> "All were armed. The two principals went at it. The two seconds looked on. Soon the two seconds began to quarrel. Finally, Mr. Hulton said something to Mr. Eastwood about the latter's principal that only blood would wash out. Mr. Eastwood fell upon Mr. Hulton and slew him. Then he rushed upon his principal's opponent and slew him. Then he picked

> up the swords of the fallen men, and he and Captain Bogle-Smith marched off the stage with their chins elevated. Then the slain picked themselves up, and everybody walked inside and partook of refreshments."
>
> – Ibid.

After the display, the audience also had the chance to handle some of the weapons, much to the delight of the young boys in attendance, who struggled to lift the two-handed swords.

The Windsor exhibition is typical of Captain Hutton's public demonstrations during this period, being in the nature of an "educational entertainment" offered to ladies and gentlemen of privilege. It was also, evidently, a good-humoured affair, complete with theatrical flourishes and mock-serious banter between the combatants.

The display also had a political dimension, however. As noted above, Hutton often referred to his concerns about the state of English military swordsmanship during his exhibitions of historical fencing. An anonymous "Special Correspondent," reviewing the Windsor display for the *Leeds Mercury* of Saturday, May 6, remarked:

> "All honour to the officers of the 1st King's Dragoon Guards and Captain Hutton, for trying to revive swordsmanship in the Army, by giving a display at Windsor cavalry barracks last Monday. I am afraid, however, that it is 'only a flash in the pan,' and that it will not have much effect on the swordsmanship of the army in general. I have myself known some commanding officers who were most enthusiastic in the encouragement and support of this important part of a soldier's training. They would contribute largely themselves, ask the officers and their friends to subscribe from time to time for the purpose of giving prizes at competitions, and defray the expenses incurred at entertainments, with the result that about half a dozen clever men would take the prizes, and other men who constantly studied and competed yearly were never fortunate enough to win anything, and at last gave up the attempt in disgust.

"Displays with rapier and dagger, buckler and broadsword, etc., are usually introduced to vary the entertainment, but the things to which greater attention should be paid in our army are fencing, broadsword play or singlestick, bayonet v. bayonet, sword v. bayonet, lance v. bayonet and v. sword. After two years' instruction in these weapons every man ought to be able fairly to hold his own against any ordinary antagonist he may be expected to meet on a campaign."

Another reviewer picked up on the same theme:

"Lord Roberts since his arrival in England has strongly pressed upon the military authorities the desirability of taking immediate steps to improve swordsmanship among the officers of the Army ... It will be interesting to know whether Captain Hutton will be sought in connection with this reform. The author of 'Cold Steel' has shown in the case of the King's Dragoon Guards what a master-mind can do to improve swordsmanship; but unfortunately master-minds are not always appreciated by red-tape officials, and there can be no amount of 'love lost' between the gymnastic staff and the author of 'Cold Steel.'"

– *Newcastle Weekly Courant*, July 22, 1893.

Meanwhile, although Captain Hutton's clique appears to have been by far the most active proponents and demonstrators of "ancient swordplay," others were working along at least broadly similar lines. Notably, French fencers were staging their own historical swordplay events. In February of 1894 the Société d'Encouragement à l'Escrime mounted an elaborate "fete de l'epee" at the Grand Hotel in Paris, which included both "serious" (competitive) and "picturesque" (historical) fencing displays in a wide range of styles.

The Austrian fencer and antiquarian Josef Schmeid-Kowarzik, an independently wealthy enthusiast of all manner of ancient swordplay, organized a number of similar exhibitions in Vienna during this period. In co-operation with the Haudegen fencing club, Schmeid-Kowarzik demonstrated the use of traditional German weapons including the dussack and two-handed sword. He was also the co-author, with Hans Kufahl, of the *Fechtbüchlein* ("Fencing Booklet"), a comprehensive survey of historical fencing schools and practices.

Back in England, Hutton's efforts attracted their share of emulation. During April of 1894, Captain Cuthbert Keeson delivered a lecture and demonstration on *Swordsmanship* at the headquarters of the Victoria and St. George's Rifles in Berkeley Square. Hutton himself was a guest at this lecture, and Captain Keeson followed Hutton's theme of deploring the state of military fencing. After a brief but "sufficiently comprehensive" history lesson, Keeson brought out an admirable collection of weapons including Indian, Japanese, Chinese, African, German, Italian and Spanish swords.

According to a reviewer from the *Daily News*:

> "In showing how knights of the Middle Ages handled (the two handed sword) with a 'long sweep,' Captain Keeson came perilously near to decapitating one of his brother officers, who was waiting to give a further illustration of two-handed sword exercise. In this bout Lieutenant Kingdon and Mr. F. Geoghegan proved that if fencing is not much practiced by the Victoria and St. George's, the members of that corps do not lack the thews and sinews for the pastime."

During one of the subsequent bouts, this time at rapiers and daggers between Captain Keeson himself and a Lieutenant Wilkinson, Keeson's blade was broken, of which incident he made adroit use by announcing that it left him a little breath with which to continue his lecture.

Combats at sword and buckler and then rapier and cloak opposed to rapier and dagger followed:

> "By a trick well known to sixteenth century duellists, Captain Keeson threw the cloak away from him, so that it turned around the point of his adversary's blade, and thus effectively the combat closed."
>
> – *Daily News*, February 7 1894.

In May, Cyril Matthey (then aged thirty), Alfred Hutton (fifty-five) and some of their young students from the L.R.B. School of Arms travelled to Brussels, Belgium to take part in a grand festival of the sword, entitled *L'Escrime a Travers les Ages*. This spectacle was held in the Royal Monnaie Opera House on May 21–22.

Their exhibitions of historical fencing, later described by Hutton himself as "the leading fighting roles," were extremely well received and, as we shall see later, may have inspired some of their French peers to pursue the practical study of historical fencing in greater earnest. As a result of their showing in Belgium, both Hutton and Matthey were named as honourary members of the Cercle d'Escrime de Bruxelles. The year 1894 also saw Hutton elected as a Fellow of the Society of Antiquaries, on the strength of his historical fencing research.

During this period, Egerton Castle appears to have concentrated primarily on his writing career. Collaborating with his wife Agnes, he produced a series of historical adventure novels in which fencing and dueling played frequent and prominent parts. Their novels were popular with the reading public and were generally wellreceived by literary critics as well.

Meanwhile, Hutton continued his research, presenting his findings via articles and lectures, which often included practical demonstrations of the various arts at his command. On April 14th he presented an exhibition of combat techniques with the greatsword, which was recorded by Graphic newspaper sketch artist Percy Macquoid as part of a six-part series entitled *Types of Swordsmanship*.

It was also in 1894 that Hutton began what was evidently a close study of George Silver's *Paradoxes of Defence*, which had been rediscovered by Mr. W. London in the British Museum's manuscript collection some four years previously.

On March 26th of 1895, the Société d'Encouragement à l'Escrime presented another fencing spectacle at the Cirque d'Ete in Paris. *L'escrime À Différentes Époques* featured a diverse range of weapons and fencing styles, tracing the development of swordplay from 1606 to contemporary foil and sabre play. The exhibition included the use of the sword and dagger, two-handed sword, and sword and buckler and also featured re-enactments of the famous Jarnac/Chataigneraie duel and the smallsword encounter between the Chevalier Saint-Georges and the Chevalière d'Eon.

In January of the following year, two of Hutton's students, Ernest Stenson Cooke and Frank Whittow, both now in their early twenties, presented a paper entitled *Swordsmanship* at Toynbee Hall in London. Assisted by the members and cadets of the London Rifle Brigade, they also performed a comprehensive demonstration of various historical fencing styles. Stenson Cooke's remark that the practice of "ancient swordplay" constituted "a most useful and fascinating exercise, and an essentially manly amusement" was well received by their large audience.

On July 6th Hutton himself delivered a lecture, *Notes on Ancient Fence,* for members of the Albany Club in Kingston-on-Thames. Held under the patronage of Prince Edward, the Albany Club presentation was held as a fund-raiser for the Royal Cambridge Asylum for Soldier's Widows. A copy of the programme notes has survived, offering us a valuable insight into the detail of this display. This elaborate programme, printed in a suitably archaic font in blue ink upon parchment-like paper, was entitled *A descriptive account of the 16th century swordplay, by members of the school of arms, London Rifle Brigade under the direction of Captain Alfred Hutton, F.S.A. and Ernest Stenson Cooke, Esq. With notes on 'Ancient Fence' by Captain A. Hutton and on the bibliography of the art of fence, by Captain C.A. Thimm, 1896, F.R.G.S.*

Hutton began the presentation with a short address:

> "Of all periods the 16th century was most prolific in 'armes blanches,' they consisted of two distinct kinds, the arms of the hand comprising various forms of swords and daggers, and the "arms of the staff" such as pikes, bills, halberds, &c, which were of course wielded with both hands, and which we may trace back to their original forms of simple wooden weapons. Of these there were three, the quarter-staff, or long staff, about eight feet in length, served as a walking staff, a leaping pole and a very formidable weapon of offence in the hands of a strong and active man; this developed into the various forms of the halberd, and we have a survival of it in the modern rifle and bayonet. Next we have 'ye short staf of convenyent length" treated of, among other arms, by George Silver at the end of the 16th century; it was a distinct walking staff, accommodated

to the powers of its owner, and reaching usually to about the height of his shoulder. In fighting it was wielded with both hands, and held at the end. From the fence of this staff was deduced that of the two-hand sword, and it remains among us still in the form of the 'great stick'—the French 'baton.'

"Thirdly we have the ordinary cudgel or stout walking stick, the 'waster' of the Elizabethan 'prentices, used of course with one hand and always accompanied in old times by the hand buckler, and we have it today as a fighting weapon, though of course without its shield, as the Irishman's blackthorn and the Frenchman's 'canne'; we see here the origin of that sword and buckler play of the gentry and their retainers, which gave birth to various fanciful sets of weapons such as the Short Sword and Dagger, case of Rapiers, Rapier and Dagger, Rapier and Cloak, &c. The wooden weapons were not 'knightly' and therefore could not be imposed upon a gentleman in the lists; they belonged entirely to the lower orders.

"Of these the cudgel is particularly interesting, being the weapon with which common fellows were obliged to void their quarrels in judicial combat; of these fights I may mention two as being recorded in history, one in the time of Henry III, between Walter Blowberne and Hamon Le Stare, who were nothing better than a pair of thieves who had fallen out about their booty; and the second, rendered famous by Olivier de la Marche, which took place at Valenciennes in the presence of Duke Phillip of Burgundy, in 1547, between two tailors named Mahuot and Jacotin Plouvier on account of a murder. Shakespeare also gives a graphic instance of such a fight in the second part of *King Henry VI,* the characters engaged being Thomas Horner, an armourer, and Peter his apprentice. These judicial encounters were resorted to in cases where accusation was made and denied on oath, and there being no witnesses on either side; the men were compelled to fight it out, the belief being that the Deity Himself would interfere and assist the innocent.

> "At this period of our Art there was absolutely no 'lunge,' it had not yet been invented; the movements of the feet were mainly 'passes' or steps forwards and backwards, and 'traverses' or lateral steps. They were effected with more or less swiftness as the occasion required; an impetuous man, indeed, would often actually charge his enemy.
>
> "An interesting feature in the defence was the 'grip,' to which recourse was had after parrying a furious charge of the opponent; it consisted of seizing his hand, hilt or wrist with the left hand, and dispatching him with a thrust, a cut, or a blow with the pommel, after which latter George Silver advises us to 'strike up his heels' as a good way of terminating the affair."

After Hutton finished his lecture, there commenced a bout at French dueling sabres between George Harvest and Frank Whittow, followed by a sabre contest between Ernest Stenson Cooke and W.P Gate. Hutton had decided to stage these bouts, fought with modern weapons, first in the programme "so as not to mar the picturesqueness of the Combats of the XVIth Century."

The initial contest of ancient fence was an exhibition of dagger and cloak combat performed by H.J. Buzzard and A. Marillier. According to Hutton's programme notes:

> "Down to the end of the Elizabethan period a dagger or sheath knife was openly worn by everyone both gentle and simple, and in those turbulent times came out of its scabbard very easily, so that a knowledge of its fighting powers was very needful. This exercise required extreme agility and watchfulness, the dagger was held point upwards with the thumb resting on the flat of the blade, and the cloak was would twice around the left arm, the collar being grasped in the hand; it was used to pary with, and if it chanced to work loose from the arm it was thrown at the enemy in such a manner as to envelop his entire person, or at least his attacking arm and weapon."

The programme announced the next bout as a contest of "Ye Sworde and Buckler fyght against ye lyke weapons":

> "Sword and Buckler is undoubtedly the most ancient style of fight, being traceable to the days of the Saxons, and in the early part of the 16th century it was in full use, and throughout that period was preferred by English swordsmen to any other kind of fight, and above all to that of the long Italian rapier, to which they had an especial objection. Our sword and buckler men observed, as we do now, certain fixed customs regarding fair play, and it was considered unmanly to strike below the knees, and the use of the point was looked upon as scarcely legitimate, so much so that some swords were made so as to render it almost impracticable; a very curious cut, given with the 'false edge' at the lower part of the ham, was regularly taught and often resorted to, notably in the fight between two Englishmen, Newton and Hamilton in the year 1547, and also in the still more famous combat between Chastaignerai and Jarnac, in the presence of Henry II of France, in which he latter was victorious, and the stroke has been known ever since as the 'Coup de Jarnac.'"

This sword and buckler combat was fought between H.F. Gaydon and R.P. Walker, and it was followed immediately by a "Twohande Sworde fyght against ye lyke weapon," performed by their colleagues Whittow and Gate:

> "The Two-hand sword was used most largely by the Swiss Infantry and, awkward as it was to handle, possessed a distinct system of fence of its own based on that of the short staff; it was the favourite weapon of our King Henry VIII, who proposed its use in the tournaments at the Field of the Cloth of Gold, but Francis 1st wisely declined it on the plea that there were no gauntlets then made sufficiently strong to guarantee the hands against accidental damage. The masters kept specially

made foil swords for the teaching of this branch of the art, and from some of them till recently in the possession of the Baron de Cosson the pair used this afternoon have been copied, and the fencing has been carefully worked up from Marozzo, di Grassi and others."

Messrs. Marillier and Buzzard took the field again for the fourth exhibition, which was a bout at "long Rapiers and Dagg'rs":

> "This sword, which was over 4 feet in length, and so cumbersome that an auxiliary weapon carried in the left hand for defensive purposes, usually the dagger, was absolutely indispensable, was of Italian origin, and its large, graceful, highly ornamented hilt, along with its deadly fighting powers, soon recommended it to the principal gentry, among whom it superseded the word and buckler, doubtless party for the reason that the little shield, although an excellent weapon of defence, was decidedly inconvenient as an item of apparel. Rapier fencing as an art improved gradually under various masters, many of whose works are still extant, until we find it at its best in that of Alfieri (1653), but about this period it began to lose its favours with the Western nations, and in France and England especially it gave place to the small sword; it held its own however in the land of its birth, and the Italian foil fencing of to-day is but a slightly modified form of the rapier play of the 17th century."

Next, Captain Hutton himself took up arms against Ernest Stenson Cooke in an exhibition of "ye Shorte Syngle Sworde Fyght against ye lyke weapon, wt ye gryppes."

> "The play of 'ye shorte sworde' I have derived from a MS. Work (by George Silver, about 1596) in the British Museum, a transcript of which, by my late friend, Mr. William London, is now, thanks to the kindness of the family, in my possession. It bears a resemblance to our modern broadsword play, of which

> it may be regarded as the direct ancestor, having been handed down to us in more improved forms by the pens of Sir W. Hope, Donald Bane, Captain Godfrey, Lonnergan, the typical master of the English Gladiators, John Taylor and Angelo; as the title suggests, the sword only was used without the assistance of either dagger or buckler, although the fighting man of that day took care, especially when he was abroad o' nights, to have his left arm protected by a stout buff 'gripping gauntlet' (guanto di presa), the palm of which was sometimes lined with fine mail.
>
> "An interesting part of the play consisted of the 'gryppes,' on the subject of which Silver is very emphatic; suffice it to say that they consisted of certain methods of overpowering the enemy's sword-hand, after having parried his fierce rushing charge. I think that these grips are worthy of at least the notice of officers and others who may some day have to do with an opponent armed with both sword and shield."

As we shall see, Hutton's interest in Silver's "gryppes" and their potential application to military sabre combat was to develop into an enduring theme.

The short sword presentation was followed by a rapier and cloak combat between George Harvest and E.A. Johnson:

> "In the early part of the 17th century the dagger began to disappear as part of the civilian costume, although the rapier, somewhat lightened in form, remained, and a means of defence against it was still needful, and to this purpose the cloak very easily adapted itself; it was carried and manipulated in the same way as in the fight of the cloak and dagger."

The sixth combat was between regular sparring partners Whittow and Gate:

> "The 'Case of Rapiers' is another curious method of fighting belonging distinctly to the 16th century, the swords were short ones like those used in buckler play, they were a perfect

> pair, and were kept together in one scabbard, they could not possibly have been worn as an article of dress, and for this reason men of the time often omitted to study their use, but they were 'knightly' weapons, and Marozzo impresses on his pupils the advantage of knowing how to wield them in case of being engaged in a duel in the lists."

There followed a mixed-weapons bout of rapier and dagger opposed to rapier and cloak, played by Marillier and Stenson Cooke:

> "In the somewhat lawless times to which all these combats belong, a man hardly ever left his house without weapons of some kind, and as has already been shewn these arms were of varied forms, it was therefore to be expected that in the case of a sudden brawl he might have to fight for his life against one carrying weapons almost in every way dissimilar to his own, we therefore give two examples of such mixed encounters. In the first of these, one has come out completely armed with rapier and dagger while the other has forgotten his dagger at home, but fortunately is carrying his cloak over his arm and, this being an excellent means of defence, the fight is after all not so very unequal."

The second mixed-weapons combat was played between R.P. Walker and H.F. Gaydon:

> "Here we must suppose a Court gallant to be taking his walk abroad armed with the fashionable rapier and poniard, when he is set upon by a more rough and ready person bearing the sword and buckler, the customary weapons of his class."

The final and most elaborate presentation was described in the programme as "Ye Duel of ye Mignons wt Rapiers and Dagg'rs" and was fought by Hutton and Stenson Cooke representing the principals, seconded by the hard-working Whittow and Harvest, with Johnson and Gate acting as "tierces":

> "In the 16th and part of the 17th centuries, it was the custom for the seconds to fight as well as the principals, and in some cases as many as six or seven were engaged on either side. It was for some time a matter of dispute among the jurisconsults of the sword, as to whether or no a combatant, who had been successful in his share of the fight, should go to the assistance of the rest of his party; these experts at last decided that it would be the depth of baseness were he to neglect to assist his friends when hard pressed, the idea of two to one being scarcely fair does not seem to have occurred to them. This custom caused the fights to assume an especially sanguinary character, each man being anxious to rid himself of his man as soon as possible lest a casualty on his own side cause odds against him. When the affair was over it was usual for the victors, after attended to the wounded of their own party, to collect all the weapons that were left lying about on the ground, and to carry them off as evidence of their success, about those fallen on the other side they gave themselves no concern whatever."

The Albany Club exhibition was a great success as both a charitable fund-raiser and as a means of raising the profile of "the Art of Fence" in England. Hutton, Matthey, Harvest and Stenson Cooke repeated the programme for an assault-at-arms event held at the Birmingham Athletic Institute in November, as a testimonial in honour of ex-Corporal Thomas Hill.

It was also during 1895 that Captain Hutton became the first President of the newly established Amateur Fencing Association, which had originated as the fencing branch of the Amateur Gymnastics Association. Throughout this period, both Hutton and Egerton Castle were working tirelessly to promote the cause of organized training and competition in the modern competitive forms of fencing; encouraging the establishment of new clubs, cultivating contacts and patrons, and drafting the panoply of regulations that were necessary to re-establish the sport in their homeland.

As the President of the new Association, Hutton continued his very vocal criticism of contemporary English military swordsmanship. In April of 1895 a new system of sabre fencing was introduced to the British Army, under the auspices of Colonel George Malcolm Fox, who was, at that time, the Inspector-General of the Army Physical Training Corps. During the preceding decade, Colonel Fox had been responsible for the construction of numerous new Army gymnasia and for the development of a systematic method of military physical training, drawing from gymnastics, calisthenics and weightlifting.

Colonel Fox had been impressed by the system of sabre fencing taught by the Italian master-at-arms Ferdinando Masiello, which he had seen during a visit to Florence in 1893. Fox then invited Masiello and his assistant, Giuseppe Magrini, to teach a course in sabre fencing for the officers and staff-sergeants at Aldershot Camp, which was the base of the Army Physical Training Corps. Masiello's system was subsequently adopted as the official method of sabre fencing instruction for all British soldiers, as outlined in a booklet, *The Infantry Sword Exercise,* which was published by the War Office in 1895.

True to form, Hutton produced a booklet the next year entitled *Criticism of the Infantry Sword Exercise of 1895*, in which he again took serious issue with the Army's new official sabre curriculum, which he viewed as being a tragic mistake and a missed opportunity. We shall address the substance and detail of this controversy in the next chapter.

In May of 1896, however, Hutton was back in the newspapers in a less truly contentious capacity, as the fight choreographer for the previously mentioned production of *Romeo and Juliet,* starring Esme Beringer. Much was made of the fact that his involvement would rescue the play from the fencing anachronisms that had been committed by previous choreographers. Hutton was quoted as saying:

> "The fighting of the Shakespearean era is so peculiarly adapted to stage display that it seems strange that it should not have been more cultivated; it may, perhaps, lack some of the refined elegance of the modern French school, but the

loss is more than counterbalanced by the varied beauty of the weapons, and the picturesque movements of the combatants. *Romeo and Juliet*, with its five distinct duels, offers a fairly wide field to the student of old sword-play."

– Alfred Hutton, "The Combats in Romeo and Juliet,"
Daily Telegraph, May 11, 1896

Hutton staged the opening brawl between the servants of the houses of Montague and Capulet with broadswords and bucklers, while the street fight between Tybalt and Benvolio was taken verbatim from *Paradoxes of Defence*, including one of Silver's "gryps," which ended the fight. Tybalt and Mercutio fought armed with paired rapiers, and then Romeo's rapier and dagger fencing overmatched Tybalt. The final fight scene, between Romeo and Paris, was likewise fought with rapiers and daggers. Critics praised the fight sequences both for their realism and for their much-touted attention to historical accuracy.

Hutton's dedication to the study and restoration of "ancient" swordsmanship had gained the respect of sportsmen and actors, but his intentions had ever gone beyond spectacle, and to the serious application of combat. In this venture, for all of the enthusiasm he found amongst military officers, and even for his command performance before the Prince of Wales, he had made little progress. But the old captain was nothing if not redoubtable, and he had two dedicated allies: the much younger Captain Cyril Matthey, and the unpublished manuscript of the equally redoubtable swordsman and critic of "fashionable new fencing," the Elizabethan gentleman, George Silver.

BOUT WITH ENGLISH BACKSWORD BY CAPTAIN HUTTON AND MR. H. SWEETMAN

Hutton's study of the old English system of backsword combat would soon have him crossing blades in lecture and print with the British Army and its new system of military swordsmanship.

Chapter 9

Sword Fighting and Sword Play (1897–8)

For the next two years, Hutton and Matthey collaborated on research into George Silver's system of fence. Hutton excerpted some of Silver's "closes and gryps" for an article appearing in the *Indian Fencing Review,* which was pointedly entitled "Sword Fighting and Sword Play."

On September 25, 1897 he demonstrated Silver's close-quarters combat as part of a comprehensive display of both historical and contemporary fencing, described in this *London Times* review:

> "A most interesting display of swordsmanship, ancient and modern, by members of the Whitton Park Club, under the direction of Alfred Hutton, F.S.A., was given in the club grounds, West Middlesex, yesterday afternoon. With the exception of one or two very slight showers the weather was favourable, and there were some 400 or 500 spectators present.
>
> "The club, which has only been opened this summer, is instituted to provide a club-house and grounds for in and out-door sports all the year round, and is admirably suited to that purpose, being easily accessible to London both by rail and road. The resident secretary is Captain C.A. Thimm,

and amongst the vice-presidents are the Earl of Mayo, the Earl of Portarlington, Captain Lord Charles Beresford, Lord Edward Spencer Churchill and Sir Henry Irving. The Sports Committee includes such well-known figures as Lieutenant-Colonel E.M. Alexander (Surrey County Gun Club), Mr. G. Lacy Hillier, Major Walter Wingfield, Captain A. Hutton and Mr. C.W. Alcock (Surrey County Cricket Club).

"The display, which was supposed to illustrate 'Ye fightes of ye sixteenth century,' was held in a special roped-off area at the back of the club-house, and was watched with keen interest. Capt. C.A. Thimm gave an exposition of dagger and cloak against similar weapons, his opponent being Mr. E.D. Johnson (London Rifle Brigade). Next Capt. A. Hutton and Mr. R. Donajowski (King's Own Regiment) had a bout with the long rapier and dagger. Mr. E. Stenson Cooke (L.R.B.) and Mr. W.P. Gate (L.R.B.) had an admirable bout with the two-handed sword, and this was followed by Capt. Thimm and Mr. R. Donajowski with sword and buckler. The display also included the use of rapier and cloak, rapier and cloak v. sword and buckler, rapier and dagger against rapier and cloak, and the 'gryps and clozes' of George Silver, a brave English gentleman of Shakespearian times.

"After a contest between Captain Hampden Wigram (Scots Guards) and Mr. Stenson Cooke (L.R.B.) with modern sabres, there was a 'Poule a l'epee' open to all members of Whitton Park Club. The entries included Capt. H. Wigram, Mr. E.D. Johnson, Mr. F.W. Whitton, Mr. W.P. Gate and Mr. E. Stenson Cooke. The winner was Mr. W.P. Gate (L.R.B.)."

Silver's close combat may also have influenced Hutton's fight choreography for the Elizabethan Stage Society's production of both *Arden of Faversham*, a play sometimes claimed, on rather slender evidence, to have been an anonymous work by William Shakespeare, and for the duel scene in *My Lady's Orchard*, featuring swordplay that a *Stage* reviewer described as being "curious."

His fight choreography for the *Three Musketeers*, however, was widely considered to be a highlight of an outstanding production:

> "The play will surely gratify the warlike Briton. It is full of fights, and everyone that's fit is frightfuller than the other. One against—two, three, four, five, six. Three against a dozen, and so-forth. A man needed to be ambidextrous, in those days. He thrust and lunged with his rapier in one hand, and parried with his deadly dagger in the other. If dagger failed he used his cape, or his great hat, or his leather gauntlet. It nearly chokes one to watch them at it in the daylight, or moonlight, or at a safe distance. There is no danger, ladies, no need to faint—the steel is button-blunted. That famous swordsman, Captain Hutton, has drilled them, which is enough for you all to know that though the play is romantic, the fighting is done with strict regard to historical accuracy."
>
> – *Daily News*, November 3, 1898.

It was also in 1898 that Hutton and Matthey published complementary books referring especially to Silver's close-quarters combat techniques, as they might be adapted for use by British soldiers. Hutton compiled several earlier works under the title *The Swordsman: A Manual of Fence and the Defence Against an Uncivilised Enemy* and Matthey published a combined edition of Silver's *Paradoxes of Defence* (1599) and the manuscript of *Bref Instructions Upon My Paradoxes of Defence* (Sloane MS No. 376, circa 1599).

Writing on "the Grips and Closes" with regards to defence against "uncivilized" enemies, Hutton began:

> "To my mind the highest type of barbarian fighting man is the Afridi, armed with his tulwar or chara, and his round shield. Now what will this Afridi do?—or rather, what will he not do? He will not politely salute you, he will not come on guard in the correct fencing-room style and abstain from attacking until the blades have been engaged, and he will not

> in his fighting make use of the lunge and recover to which we civilised swordsmen are accustomed, for the very good reason that he knows nothing about these things; but what he must and will do is exactly what our English sword and buckler men did in the days of Shakespeare, at which time the lunge had not yet been invented. He will advance or retire, more or less quickly as suits his purpose, with steps or 'passes' as in walking or running, he will 'traverse' or move round you in a circle, looking out for a chance to come in, or he will rush you, with a furious charge, his blows being mostly oblique downward strokes, and when attacked he will either parry with his shield and strike at the same time, or he will 'fly out,' i.e., jump out of the way; and this is a style of fencing to which we nineteenth-century fencers are not much accustomed, so we must go back to our Elizabethan ancestors to find the best means of combatting such tactics."

After introducing his readers to the works of George Silver and pointedly remarking that "those old masters taught fighting, we teach nothing but fencing nowadays," Hutton proceeded to describe four grips for use against those opponents who would not play by the rules of the salle d'armes:

> "GRIP I.
>
> The enemy charges you with an oblique downward cut at your left shoulder.
>
> Parry high prime. Advance your left foot, and pass your left hand, the thumb being downwards, and the back of your hand to your right, under your own sword and seize his sword hand or wrist, forcing it downwards and drawing it in towards your left side.
>
> Actions of the sword:-
>
> Very promptly deal him a strong blow on the right side of his head with your pummel.

Throw back your right shoulder so as to prevent his seizing your sword arm, and give him a thrust or cut in the high lines, or, if his lower parts are more open, the coup de jarnac will be found very effective.

"GRIP II.

On the same attack parry quarte, step in and seize his wrist underneath, forcing it a little upwards to your own left.

Actions of the sword:-

Drop the point of the sword to the rear over your left shoulder, and give him the pummel on his forehead.

Draw back your right shoulder to prevent his gripping you, and use your point or edge where he is most open.

Pass your point over his left shoulder in such a way that the blade will be in a transverse position behind him with the false edge against the back of his neck, and draw your sword strongly towards you.

"GRIP III:

The enemy charge you with an oblique downwards cut at your right shoulder.

Parry tierce. Pass forward your left foot, seize his hilt or wrist with your left hand and force his sword arm upwards to your own right, thus deviating his shield from the line of defence.

Actions of the sword:-

Thrust or cut him, not forgetting your coup de jarnac, where he is most open, which will be underneath.

Having seized him as above, force his hand downwards to your right, and thrust or cut him in the upper lines.

Having seized him as above, force his sword hand to your own left, and, acting as after the quarte parry and seizure, cut, thrust or give the pummel as may be convenient. Should

> he drop his shield and come in to grapple with you, then lean quickly, pass your sword behind your back, leaning your wrist against your left side, and present your point at his belly.
>
> "GRIP IV.
>
> Your enemy charges you and cuts low at the left side, leg, or fork.
>
> Parry septime, seize his wrist from above, carrying his sword hand to your left, and cut or thrust him as is most convenient.
>
> Parry low prime, seize from above, and strike him an upward blow with your pummel underneath his chin.
>
> An attack in the low line to the right is to be parried with seconde and answered with a riposte; gripping is unadvisable here, as it tends to upset your own equilibrium."

After quoting Silver to the effect that these grips should not be attempted unless the adversary himself forced the issue at close quarters, Hutton concluded:

> "I cannot help thinking that to those whose conditions of service imposes upon them the probability of meeting with warriors of the barbarian type a certain knowledge of wrestling would be useful—a man in Silver's time was hardly looked upon as a complete swordsman without it. A vast amount of fuss is made in the Army nowadays about boxing, but wrestling appears to have been entirely ignored."

It is difficult not to read Hutton's critical comments as being directed primarily towards Colonel G. Malcolm Fox, who had been responsible for introducing Ferdinando Masiello's sabre fencing system into the Army and who advocated boxing training for soldiers (as did Hutton himself). As previously noted, the official adoption of Masiello's system had aroused a storm of controversy, particularly amongst those British fencers who were loyal to the French system, and it was Captain Hutton who spearheaded the most public and vehement criticism. Colonel Fox's decision had flown in the face of Hutton's campaign to have the Army adopt his own system, and given that the lives of British soldiers could literally be at stake, sentiment on this issue ran very high. Hutton's scrapbook eventually contained no less than one hundred and eight press clippings relating to the *Infantry Sword Exercise* controversy, collected from a variety of newspapers and journals in under six months.

Both sides of the debate had their advocates. Here is a typical offering from an anonymous "Special Correspondent" for the Military Notes column of the *Leeds Mercury*:

> "The vexed question as to which method of infantry sword exercise is best (Italian or French) has not yet been fully decided. I am inclined, however, to think that the Adjutant-General (after carefully weighing the merits of both systems, and having decided in favour of the Italian as taught by M. Masiello) will not be disposed to throw aside the lately issued official *Infantry Sword Exercise* and revert to the old system. Mr. Alfred Hutton, late Captain 1st Dragoon Guards, and himself a fencer of some repute, says that Masiello's system is more suited to prepare pupils for duelling with light, flimsy swords than for teaching true swordsmanship with fairly heavy swords, such as are used by our infantry. It should also be borne in mind that the latter are absolutely necessary in the case of our troops who have to defend themselves from attacks by savage or half-civilised foes in various parts of the Empire, such as India, South Africa, or the Soudan.
>
> "Mr Hutton condemns the "on guard" position as being most fatiguing, and in this he is certainly right, for no man can keep his sword arm quite straight and up to the height of his shoulder for many minutes without feeling 'ready to drop,' except as the result of very long and constant training. The 'lunge' is also very faulty, because of the over-balanced position, and the difficulty in quickly recovering so as to be able to defend one's self. So also is the 'jump' when attacking,

which is most unnatural, and indeed almost impossible, seeing that out soldiers usually have to defend their lives on rough ground, and encumbered by belts, accoutrements and heavy boots. Further practical objections to the Italian system could easily be pointed out, if space permitted.

"IS THE MASIELLO SYSTEM FITTED FOR OUR SWORDS?

"Now for an 'onlooker's' arguments in favour of the new system of teaching. It is presumed that the Adjutant-General and Colonel Fox, superintendant of the Gymnasium at Aldershot, have both been trained in the French system of fencing, etc. as indeed all our officers have hitherto been, and that therefore they would feel inclined to favour that system. After repeated trials and competitions between the French and Italian swordsmen, the latter have obtained the largest number of points, and have therefore clearly had the advantage.

"The Masiello lunge, owing to the swordsman leaning forward from the hips as much as possible, reaches ten or twelve inches farther than the French, as in the latter case you are taught to keep the body back. This is an advantage, no doubt, if the recovery to the 'guard' position is easy. The 'on guard' position, with a straight arm in line with the shoulder, can be attained as easily as the bent arm position with the elbow down to the waist, and the advantage of it is recognised by both the French and the Germans, who say it was impossible to escape from the point always presented to them. From this it would appear that the Masiello system is the best, if it can be used in the field with heavy swords as well as with the light, narrow swords and foils used in the fencing room. Another argument in favour of the Italian system is that at the International Fencing Tournament this week in Paris, the 2nd prize for foils, and 1st and 2nd prizes for sabres (professionals) and also the first and second prizes (amateurs) were carried off by the Italians."

– *Leeds Mercury*, June 13 1896.

Hutton's original military sabre system, as presented in *Cold Steel* some six years earlier, had also recommended an Italian, rather than French, system and, like Masiello, he had specifically commended his readers to use lightweight sabres for training purposes, those being "capable of more varied treatment than the cumbersome weapons in vogue in our English schools."

Hutton's objection against Masiello's system was not on grounds of sentiment, nor nationalistic loyalty, but was rather (at least largely) based on the practical points outlined in his *Criticism* essay and in the chapter from *Swordsmanship* reproduced above. Over the preceding several years, Hutton's own system had been significantly revised towards greater combative realism, simplicity and the inclusion of close-quarters combat techniques inspired by George Silver's methods. Masiello's system had been adopted into the Army's physical education programme verbatim, and had not been subject to similar revision.

Captain Cyril Matthey's introduction to his republication of Silver's works provides further insight into the nature and aims of the project he had undertaken with Hutton. Matthey carefully distinguished between the different types of fencing required in the salle d'armes, on the dueling field and on the treacherous terrain of the battlefield, also noting that while duels had been outlawed in England for many years, an Englishman travelling abroad might still be challenged to defend his honour with cold steel. Indicating that the newly-authorized British Army system of sabre fencing was closely based on a stylized classical dueling style—a thinly-veiled reference to Masiello's system—Matthey advocated instead for:

> "... a simple system ... to teach an officer how to defend himself thoroughly, and how to attack an adversary, without puzzling (the officer) with a number of complicated parries and movements, which, even if practicable with a feather-weight duelling sabre, and in the fencing-room, become utterly impossible with the regulation sword, and in a fight of the 'rough and tumble' order.
>
> "(...) Why not, therefore, having decided upon the pattern of the regulation sword, have drawn up, or have caused to be drawn up, by one or more of our well known swordsmen,

competent from experience to judge what is really requisite for the purpose, a simple common-sense method of sword-fighting suitable for service requirements. This could easily be taught, and devoid of a great deal of that preliminary fencing-room drudgery that so frequently proves to be the real bar to further interest and improvement except in the case of the enthusiast—a system, in fact, of such a description that the advanced "science" of the sword is as far as possible eliminated from it, in order to make way for the simple development of individual coolness and quickness by such means as can without difficulty be practised by officers among themselves at any time.

"(...) I suggest that sword **fighting** is not taught, and that it ought to be. Fencing should be encouraged to the utmost, but fighting should be regarded, as it was by Silver, as a distinct subject, and of much greater importance in the majority of cases."

– Captain Cyril G. R. Matthey,
The Works of George Silver, 1898.

The newspaper commentators' reduction of the argument to a question of French vs. Italian fencing styles rather missed the point. Both Hutton and Matthey were, in fact, proposing a radically innovative system of saber fighting, distinct from the academic, dueling or even standard military fencing of either the French or Italian masters. Significantly, their method incorporated major elements from English systems of "ancient swordplay" including both 18th-century backswordsmanship and George Silver's method of gryps and closes. They were also, very clearly, implying that they were the men to implement this course of instruction within the army. In fact, it seems evident that by 1898 Hutton, in particular, had been chafing at the perceived missed opportunities of fencing instruction at the Aldershot military school for several decades. It is probably impossible, at this remove, to disentangle their professional ambitions from their undoubtedly genuine faith in their proposed system. Whatever the case, their cries to native Englishmen to take up the "ancient manner" of arms proved little more effective than Silver's had, three hundred years earlier.

Meanwhile, and by way of contrast, Egerton and Agnes Castle continued to go from success to success as writers of romantic historical novels. Their first "smash hit" in the literary world, *The Pride of Jennico*, was published in 1898, and they produced one major novel per year for many years thereafter. A number of their stories were dramatized for the stage in England, the USA, Canada, Australia and New Zealand. Castle's involvement in theatre also included further work as a fight choreographer. In 1899 his exciting duel scene for a production of *In Days of Old*, a play by George Alexander at St. James's Theatre, was described by one critic as being "admirable, life-like and convincing."

While Egerton Castle maintained his interest in and practice of fencing, training at the London Fencing Club and staging fight scenes as often as his writing and travel schedule allowed, he remained largely absent from the world of "ancient swordplay" for the next several years. In the meantime, however, other players were to bring fresh material into the ever-widening body of martial arts knowledge—this time, not from the past, but from a mysterious archipelago half-way around the world.

Historical fencing and Bartitsu exhibitions at the Bath Club, including an eclectic mix of boxing, savate, cane fighting, and jiujitsu, would provide Hutton a home for his circle of "ancient swordsmen."

Chapter 10

The Headquarters of Ancient Swordplay: The Bartitsu Club (1899–1902)

It was in March of 1899 that Alfred Hutton is first recorded as having worked with Edward William Barton-Wright, who had recently returned to London after three years in Japan. Barton-Wright shared Hutton's enthusiasm for all manner of close-combat methods, and was endeavoring to promote his newly-founded eclectic method of civilian self defence, which he referred to as *Bartitsu*. This name was a portmanteau of his own surname and "jiujitsu"—he was to define it as meaning "self defence in every form." The Japanese unarmed combat art comprised a significant proportion of Barton-Wright's method, which also included boxing, kicking and a unique method of self-defense with a walking stick or umbrella.

Hutton and Barton-Wright shared the stage in a demonstration performed for members of the prestigious Bath Club, so named for its indoor swimming pool—a great novelty in 1899. Hutton and his students displayed Elizabethan fencing, while Barton-Wright and his assistant lectured and exhibited their unarmed combat skills:

> "For the encouragement of the arts that foster skill in arms and physical prowess, fair friends of members assembled in great numbers at the Bath Club, on Thursday. Ordinarily the well known institution is a favourite haunt of athletic men

only, but this was 'Ladies Night,' and they took full advantage of it to fringe the galleries and margin of the swimming-bath with their gayest evening costumes. Their main object in being there was to see a demonstration of Bartitsu, and hear its principles expounded by Mr. Barton-Wright. But that did not come until near the end of a varied programme, and meanwhile spectators had to be content with exhibitions of Elizabethan swordplay.

"Many peculiarities of ancient fence were admirably illustrated by Captain Alfred Hutton and some of his pupils, with members of the Bath Club. With sword against buckler, Mr. Malcolm Fraser and Mr. Johnson, of the London Rifle Brigade engaged. Then came a bout with rapiers, or the game of two swords, between Capt. Matthey and Mr. Stenson-Cooke, L. R. B., followed by a practical lesson in wielding the two-handed sword, at which Mr. Cooke and his frequent opponent, Mr. Gate L. R. B., proved themselves very expert. After this Captain Hutton and Mr. W. H. Grenfell engaged with rapiers and daggers. In all these exercises the combatants displayed not only dexterous swordsmanship, but the easy grace of movement that is the most cherished accomplishment of those who have learned to fence.

"An impromptu exhibition of scientific swimming and floating, by Mr. Henry, gave vast entertainment for Mr. Henry, who is the author of the Badminton book on that art, illustrates it practically even better than he writes about it, which is saying a great deal.

"Still more entertaining, especially to the visitors, was a bout with gloves between the club's boxing professor and Dr. Charles Higgens. It was wonderful to see with what energy and determination the distinguished eye specialist went for his doughty opponent, taking hard knocks with the best of good humour, and returning them like a skilful fractioned in the noble art.

"After more fencing with rapiers and cloaks, and an illustration by Captain Hutton of novel methods in which a sword may be used with effect, Mr. Barton-Wright appeared on the stage.

"Unfortunately, however, he was suffering from a sprained knee, and therefore, the promised bout between him and Mr. Chipchase, an amateur champion of Cumberland wrestling, had to be postponed. Mr. Wright's accident, however, had not deprived him of all power to perform astounding feats. With Mr. Sweet as a subject to experiment upon, he showed what could be done by a quick and ready application of scientific principles against superior physical force. His system, which he calls Bartitsu, is based on knowledge of the weak parts of human anatomy. His 'locks,' devised to meet all possible forms of attack, are so effective that when put into operation by an expert they bear on the weak part in a way which the strongest man is powerless to resist. By tricks that seemed simplicity itself the demonstrator easily overcame all Mr. Sweet's strenuous efforts, and in fact made use of them to his own ends. He seemed to be able to throw the heavier man when and how he pleased, so that mere brute strength would count for little in a struggle on these terms, and the victory must inevitably be with the man who was quickest in getting the right hold. What a bout between Mr. Wright and a really good wrestler would be the spectators had no opportunity of judging, but he has promised to give a public entertainment at St. James's Hall soon, and as he invited all those present that night to be his guests on the next occasion, he is sure of a good house, for the Bath Club members and their friends were enthusiastic in their admiration of the novel adaptation of principles that have been practiced for ages by Japanese wrestlers to the art of self-defence."

– "Self Defence Against the Strong: 'Bartitsu' at the Bath Club," *London Daily News,* March 3, 1899

A little later that year, Barton-Wright established a full-time training centre, the Bartitsu School of Arms and Physical Culture, in London's Shaftesbury Avenue. Captain Hutton and some of his students from the London Rifle Brigade immediately began holding classes in both modern and historical fencing at the Bartitsu Club. Barton-Wright wrote an article for the *Black and White Budget* magazine in October 1900, describing their classes in "fencing, duelling-sword, Italian swordplay and Elizabethan swordplay ... principally in order to assist actors in rendering the different methods of ancient swordplay upon the stage correctly." It is likely that their students from the theatrical fraternity would have included Esme Beringer, George Silver (an actor who shared the name of the Elizabethan fencing master) and young Charlie Sefton. Hutton was also keeping his hand in as a stage fight choreographer during this period, devising a realistic duel scene for an Elizabethan Stage Society production of *Hamlet*.

In his revised introduction for a re-publication of *Old Sword Play* (1901), Hutton was moved to describe the Bartitsu Club as "the headquarters of ancient swordplay in this country."

Barton-Wright's Club was organized on the model of the traditional English gentlemen's club, so that prospective members had to apply to join or be recommended by existing members and then be approved by a panel including Alfred Hutton, who also served on the Club's Board of Directors. The other board members included notables such as Lord Alwyne Compton, the Hon. Herbert J. Gladstone, and Colonel G. Malcolm Fox, the former Inspector-General of the Army Physical Training Corps and Hutton's adversary in the military sabre controversy. There seem to be no records detailing the inner workings of the Bartitsu Club's Board of Directors, but it is tempting to speculate that either Captain Hutton and Colonel Fox had buried the hatchet by this time, or that their Board meetings must have been prickly affairs.

Although Barton-Wright's conception of Bartitsu evolved considerably between 1898 and 1902, it was clearly intended as a cross-training process between the variety of martial arts and combat sports taught at the Club. He also insisted that new members of the Club undertake a series of private lessons before joining in the group classes, which included a form of circuit training in which small groups of students rotated between instructors in the various component skills of Bartitsu.

Whether this cross-training process would technically have included Hutton's historical fencing classes, at least as regards the general membership, is doubtful; Barton-Wright was adamant that Bartitsu was intended for practical self defence, which, on the surface, would tend to discount training in skills such as rapier and dagger fencing. Likewise, whereas duels of honour were still being fought in some countries on the European continent, the last fatal duel in England had taken place some fifty years earlier, and fencing was widely regarded as being obsolete as a means of civilian self defence. The wearing of swords was long out of fashion, hence Barton-Wright's pragmatic solution of offering classes in self defence with walking sticks and umbrellas. However, there is evidence of collaboration between Barton-Wright and his Bartitsu instructors and Hutton's historical fencing group, and it is not unlikely that members of the Club would have enjoyed Hutton's classes on a purely recreational basis.

An article on historical fencing co-authored by Ernest Stenson Cooke and Frank Whittow appeared later that year in the *Proceedings of the Society of Antiquaries of London*, crediting both men as being members of both the London Rifle Brigade and the Bartitsu Club.

In May of 1900 the Club was represented in an Assault-at-Arms held to benefit Guy's Hospital:

> "M. Vigney (sic) and Mr. Collard, two of Mr. Barton-Wright's instructors, gave an exhibition of 'Bartitsu' walking-stick play. Everybody had heard of this new defence and offence, but it was a revelation to the audience to see the splendid development, the dexterity and quickness, and even grace, of the exponents of this really wonderful science. A striking feature of the training is that in all the exercises the pupil must become ambidextrous; in fact, the rapid transference of the walking-stick from one hand to the other was, to the uninitiated at least, one of the most powerful factors in offence and defence, and one likely to prove most puzzling to the opponent.
>
> "After another round in the fencing competition, Captain Hutton brought forward two of the 'Bartitsu' Club fencing instructors, Messrs. Collard and Rolt, who gave a display of

Elizabethan fencing, using first of all sword and buckler, and then, the more stately rapier and dagger.

"The two styles were essentially different in all but attitude. Neither man came 'on guard' with the stilted style of modern foil play. Crouching at either end of the ring, they crept towards one another like tigers, and sprang in and out, thrusting and guarding with lightning rapidity. From a spectacular point of view these contests were superb; but it was unpleasantly obvious that 'an affair of honour' in Raleigh's time was not a matter to be entered upon lightly, and certainly not a matter from which either party could hope to escape unscathed."

– *Guy's Hospital Gazette*, Volume 14, 1900

In this instance, Mr. Collard is described as having represented both Bartitsu stick fighting and historical fencing, demonstrating that at least one member of the Club cross-trained between these styles.

On June 21st, a similar but more elaborate presentation was offered to the Society of Antiquaries:

"An adjournment was then made to the library, where an exhibition of fence of the sixteenth and early seventeenth centuries was given by Captain Hutton, Mr. Guy Laking, Captain Stenson Cooke, and Messrs. F. H. Whitlow (sic), Harvey, and Percy Rolt.—The fence exhibited consisted of (1) dagger and cloak; (2) sword and buckler; (3) case of rapiers, or the fight of the two swords; (4) rapier and dagger; (5) the "gryps and clozes" of George Silver (1599); (6) rapier and cloak; and (7) the two-hand sword."

– *The Antiquary: A Magazine Devoted to the Study of the Past*, Volume 36, 1900

For his part, Captain Hutton was evidently a keen observer, and probably also a student, of the novel arts of defence presented at the Club. He wrote a short monograph on jiujitsu for schoolboys, likely based on the classes offered by Barton-Wright and/or his young Bartitsu Club colleagues, Yukio Tani and Sadakazu Uyenishi. Curiously, as well as describing some sixteen basic jiujitsu self defence techniques, Hutton's monograph also included a single technique from a Dutch unarmed combat manual written by Nicolaes Petter in 1670.

"Ancient combat" persisted upon the London stage during this period, in various guises. One of the most unusual examples is that of "Professor Sulivian," who performed at the Oxford Music Hall during June of 1900. The Professor claimed, among other accomplishments, to have fought several hundred successful duels with the dagger, sword and rapier, and to have secured the Hamburg silver cross for fencing against "forty-one of the leading swordsmen of the Continent" in a gruelling contest lasting three quarters of an hour. Professor Sulivian was accompanied by a young lady billed as Peto Aranka, the Champion Swordswoman of the Academy of Rome, of whom it was claimed that she had defeated every officer who had ever faced her with rapier and dagger.

Their act included both ordinary fencing in the Italian style and what was described as "trick fencing," which included the Professor fencing a bout while watching his opponent's reflection in a small mirror held in his left hand. He then fought a bout while seemingly blindfolded. A contest with apparently sharp sabres and then both single and double daggers followed, the Professor exciting some comment from the audience when he "all but stripped to the waist" due to heavy perspiration and then proceeded to accidentally stab himself in the foot while demonstrating that their weapons were, indeed, sharp. He finished by partially removing Miss Aranka's bodice to show that she, too, had been wounded during the display, to the consternation of their audience.

It is diverting to imagine the reaction of either Hutton or Castle to such an exhibition in the name of fencing.

On Tuesday, June 6 of 1901, Egerton Castle and his student, the actress Esme Beringer, enacted a historical swordplay sketch at a grand assault-at-arms staged in celebration of the second anniversary of the Actors' Sword Club. This institution, also referred to as the Foil Club, was based at the Salle Bertrand, 10 Warwick Street. After a days' competition in fencing with the epee and in both the Italian and French styles of foil play, Castle assumed the role of an Elizabethan era fencing master while Miss Beringer played his student. The sketch was described as being "the most interesting feature in an attractive programme," with Esme Beringer's rapier and dagger fencing being noted as displaying "remarkable grace and agility, considering the rather heavy weapons used." Three months later, Miss Beringer appeared at the Palace Theatre in an educational display entitled *Rapier and Dagger; or, the Art of Fencing Three Hundred Years Ago,* this time partnered by the actor, George Silver.

It was also in 1901 that Captain Hutton published what was to be his final major work on historical fencing, which was entitled *The Sword and the Centuries: or, Old Sword Days and Old Sword Ways.* This book was less technical than *Old Sword Play,* being more in the nature of a survey of swords and fencing styles over five centuries, illustrated with colourful accounts of famous and infamous duels. Hutton also included a glowing review of the stick fighting method taught by Bartisu Club instructor Pierre Vigny:

> "... a professor from Switzerland, who unites in himself the qualities of a champion player and of a careful, judicious teacher of his art, and he possesses in a marked degree the natural gift of facility in interesting his pupil in the work which that pupil has set himself to learn.
>
> "The instrument he employs is nothing more than the ordinary walking-stick of daily life, say for example a lightly-mounted malacca cane. The exercise, when played merely as a game, is a remarkably attractive one, so brilliant, indeed, that our time honoured English singlestick is not to be compared with it. In the first place, the player is not hampered with a buffalo or wicker hand-guard, a fact which of itself lends variety to the play, for the man can, and does, frisk his cane, about from one hand to the other, so that his opponent can never precisely tell which hand will deliver the attack, and careful practice of the various lessons will shortly make the student pretty nearly ambidextrous. One of the fist things to understand in such play as this is to preserve the hand which holds the weapon, a thing which an occasional tap on the knuckles impresses on one's memory. M. Vigny does not confine himself to teaching

a mere exhilarating game of play; he shows his pupils also the more serious side of the system, instructing them carefully in what they should do if attacked by a gang of ruffians. But we must not enter the arena of technical detail; it is better left in the hands of M. Vigny himself."

– Captain Alfred Hutton,
The Sword and the Centuries, 1901.

In November, Hutton enthusiastically demonstrated his proficiency at Bartitsu stick fighting for a *Sydney Morning Herald* interviewer:

> "In a moment the captain was holding his walking stick in such a threatening manner that the interview seemed likely to come to an abrupt conclusion.
>
> "'You see,' he went on, smiling, 'the thing has far more possibilities than you might imagine. Walking-stick play, as taught by M. Vigny, for instance, is an extremely useful bit of knowledge. Now try to hit me on the head.'
>
> "We tried. As soon as the coals had been picked out of our hair, and the lower portion of our waistcoat had been removed from our collar, the captain cheerfully resumed:
>
> "'If you are mobbed, you observe, the great thing is never to raise your hand to strike. Always keep it low. Hold your stick at each end, and thrust the first man on the mark (the solar plexus region), the second in the throat, clear a circle round you rapidly, and ...'
>
> "But the audience had fled. It is not a healthy thing to pretend to be a mob when Captain Hutton demonstrates 'a little of the art of self defence,' and it was to a prostrate form upon the sofa that the captain addressed his last remarks."

Hutton's other remarks during that interview included a return to his familiar critique of the state of military sabre instruction and some interesting comments on the subject of affairs of honor:

> "'Look at the way (the English authorities) abolished duelling, and left us helpless, with nothing in its place. In these days a scoundrel may run off with a girl, and the law does nothing except punish you if you thrash him. Now, in the old days'—and the captain strode among his weapons with the light of battle in his eyes—'it was not possible for a man to offer you a gross affront merely because he thought he could do it safely. With the fear of the duel before him he kept in his place. A row in the street or in a drawing-room is out of the question; legal methods are no remedy. The consequence is that the commonest methods of established courtesy are rapidly becoming obsolete. Are we the better for that?'"

Evidently, Hutton would have agreed with American author Robert A. Heinlein, whose 1942 science fiction novel *Beyond this Horizon* included the quote, "an armed society is a polite society. Manners are good when one may have to back up his acts with his life."

As of the present writing, there are unconfirmed reports that E.W. Barton-Wright may have borrowed from the "ancient swordplay" repertoire in developing his personal form of Bartitsu, particularly from a "1570 manual of swordsmanship," which may be a reference to Giacomo di Grassi's *True Arte of Defence* (first published in Italian in 1570, translated and published in English in 1594). Hutton would certainly have been familiar with di Grassi's work and might well have shared it with Barton-Wright. The latter's initial self-defense article for *Pearson's Magazine* had included a technique whereby an otherwise unarmed defender could defeat a dagger-wielding attacker by entangling him in the defender's overcoat, used in much the same manner as an Elizabethan-era rapier fencer would use his cloak, then execute a boxing punch and a jujitsu throw and restraint hold. Unfortunately, we do not yet know the details of this alleged influence of ancient swordplay upon Bartitsu.

As it happened, the Bartitsu bubble was soon to burst. In early 1902, the Bartitsu Club closed its doors for the last time; subsequent speculation had it that the tuition fees and enrollment fees had been too high. It is also likely that Barton-Wright had simply over-estimated the number of well-heeled

Londoners who shared his passion for exotic self-defence systems. Although he was rumoured to have continued to teach aspects of Bartitsu privately into the 1920s, Barton-Wright's moment in the sun had passed, and he spent the remainder of his career working as a physical therapist.

Bartitsu itself might have been entirely forgotten, if not for a cryptic reference in one of Sir Arthur Conan Doyle's "Sherlock Holmes" mysteries. In *The Adventure of the Empty House* (1903), Holmes explained that he had defeated his arch-nemesis, the evil Professor Moriarty, in hand-to-hand combat at the brink of Reichenbach Waterfall through his use of "baritsu (*sic*), or Japanese wrestling." It is likely that Doyle had copied the reference verbatim from a report on a Bartitsu exhibition published in the London Times during 1901, which likewise misspelled the name of the art as "baritsu" and which was subtitled "Japanese wrestling at the Tivoli."

Barton-Wright's young assistant instructors and associates dispersed, many going on to successful independent careers as professional wrestlers and/or self-defence tutors. By this time, Captain Alfred Hutton was sixty-three years old and was, perhaps, beginning to slow down; although he continued to present exhibitions for some years thereafter, the closure of the Bartitsu Club appears to have marked the end of his active teaching of ancient swordplay.

An aging Alfred Hutton demonstrates rapier and dagger fencing.

Chapter 11

Drawing to a Close (1902–08)

In February of 1902, possibly very shortly after the Bartitsu Club had ceased operations, Hutton and Castle were involved in an illustrated lecture given for members of the Playgoers' Club, on the subject of *Stage Fighting.* Their student, the actress/swordswoman Esme Beringer chaired the lecture and attendance by Club members and interested friends was described as being "phenomenal."

In introducing Captain Hutton, Miss Beringer remarked that it was quite something to have an expert's opinion on the subject, and announced that he purposed to give a practical, as well as verbal, demonstration of ancient swordplay. Captain Hutton began:

> "Miss Chairwoman (I hope that's right), and brother and sister playgoers, in the few remarks I am going to make I shall certainly go for certain things in the fighting line that I have seen done on the stage. I do not wish, however, to hurt anyone's feelings or tread on anyone's toes, wherefore I will mention no man's name; but, if my cap fits the head of any gentleman present, by all means let him wear it—it is his affair and none of mine.

> "We very often see produced on the stage plays representing various periods of the world's history, in which fighting of some sort occurs, and when such a fight is correctly played, and with weapons suitable to its period, it certainly adds much to the attraction of the piece. But how very seldom it is that we see the characters armed with the proper weapons, and how still more seldom do we see any attempt at using them as they were used in their own time."

Hutton proceeded into a typically thorough and accurate precis of the development of swordsmanship since the 15th century, noting that the play of the two-handed sword was very similar to that of the Scottish claymore, and that he would like to see that weapon, used correctly, in the stage combat between Macduff and Macbeth. In referring to George Silver, Hutton carefully distinguished between Silver, the Elizabethan authority on swordplay, and his co-incidental namesake, the young actor who was to perform in the forthcoming exhibition.

In addressing sword and buckler play, Hutton noted that it was, in his view, the ideal style in which to stage the opening brawl between the servants of the houses of Montague and Capulet in *Romeo and Juliet*, and also the fight between the characters Jack Cade and Alexander Iden in *King Henry VI*. Extending his topic into fencing with the long rapier, Hutton offered the information that, in his revived form of rapier free-play, only the point was used, and also informed the audience that he possessed antique rapier and dagger foils (training weapons, buttoned and blunted for safety).

Hutton warmed to the subject of rapier and dagger foils, particularly in connection to the famous duel scene in Hamlet:

> "Clearly Shakespeare intended that fencing bout to be played with those weapons, they were the fashionable arms of his day, and his Hamlet and Laertes being courtly personages, would naturally understand the use of them. Oh, that poor Hamlet! How absurd the actor-managers do make him look in the fencing scene. Of course, it is always the actor-manager who plays the title role, and, as a general rule, he is perfectly

innocent of anything connected with the art dimicatory; but he has got to fence, and with foils, too. Foils are talked about in the play, so he hies him to a fencing-master and asks to see some foils. The worthy professor, whose only idea of a foil is the modern one he is in the habit of using, immediately produces some specimens. Our actor-magager is delighted; he has got his foils, and he proceeds to take a dozen or so lessons in the use of them. Thus equipped he puts his fencing scene on the stage; he makes his Hamlet and Laertes, dressed in the costume of the time of Elizabeth, use the foils of that of our present Gracious Sovereign King Edward VII. This is simply burlesquing the scene, and he might as well complete the burlesque by filling the golden goblet intended for Hamlet from a magnum of Perrier Jouet.

"I have in my mind an actor-manager who put on Hamlet a while ago. This gentleman was a bit of an epicure. He says to himself, "None of your modern foils for me; no, no. I'll have rapiers—real rapiers—but what the dickens is a rapier? I'm not quite sure." So he trots off to a shop where they sell fencing requisites. He says to the young man at the counter, "Oh, er—could you by any chance show me some rapiers?" The young man replies, "Yes, sir, certainly, sir," and forthwith lays before him a few pairs of modern French duelling swords—buttoned ones, of course—and our actor-manager selects some. But, having achieved his 'rapiers,' he does not know what to do with them, any more than the other gentleman did with his foils; so he puts himself, as he thinks, into quite the right hands—he repairs to an elderly professor, whose boast is that he has taught all the principal Hamlets in the last quarter of a century—and he taught every man jack of them wrong. And now we get on the stage—no we don't, we get into the stalls, and what do we see? We see Osric or somebody bring in a bundle of highly-nickelled French fencing swords of the most up-to-date pattern, of which the Hamlet and the Laertes select each one, and they commence operations by going through, rather indifferently,

> the thoroughly modern performance of what is known as the 'Academy Salute.' Now, no such thing as a salute with the foils was known at all until the time of the first of the Angelos, in whose famous book (1783) you will find it depicted; but that, old as it now is, was not the salute put before us—what we saw was the very latest invention of the nineteenth century. This performance again verged so strongly on the burlesque that I was a little surprised that our actor-manager did not complete it by wearing on his head, instead of the flat black cap of the traditional Hamlet, a tall white hat with a black band round it. That would have completed the thing."

It is tempting to read Captain Hutton's barbed comments as a critique of the fight choreography of Baptiste Bertrand (?-1898), who had been one of Hutton's chief rivals in this sphere. Bertrand had been an elegant and experienced fencing master in his own right, but his stage fights were, to Hutton's purist sensibilities, intolerably anachronistic.

Captain Hutton continued his lecture with references to the case of rapiers, complimenting Esme Beringer for her use of that difficult weapon combination in *Romeo and Juliet*, and then finished with a brief discussion of the smallsword, noting that its play was similar to that of the modern foil except that it retained certain "tricks of the rapier-men," such as the use of the left hand in parries, disarms and seizures.

He concluded:

> "I am much gratified to be able to say that, with one or two exceptions, the lady and the gentlemen who are assisting me in the fencing bouts tonight are young members of the theatrical profession. It is to the young actors and the young actresses that we must look for improvement in stage fighting.
>
> "And now, brother and sister playgoers, a truce to talking. Let us have deeds, not words; so I will call on my friends Major Matthey and Mr. Mansfield to show you how a sudden quarrel was arranged in the days of Good Queen Bess."

Matthey and Mansfield then took the stage, armed with sword and buckler and sword and dagger, respectively. Their display was described by one critic as lacking "the fire and vehemence expected in an impromptu fight between two impassioned men," perhaps suggesting that, despite its theatrical context, it was more in the nature of an academic bout than the critic would have liked.

Captain Stenson Cooke evidently being unavailable, Matthey then engaged with Captain F.E. Whittow at two-handed swords, with Whittow emerging as the victor. It is unclear as to whether their combat was an actual fencing match or a pre-arranged set play, though Hutton's earlier comments on this subject suggest the latter.

Major Matthey was again paired with Mansfield in a rapier and cloak combat, and by this time they had evidently warmed to the task, for this bout was described as being an "exciting fight." Whittow and Mansfield were opponents in an exhibition of combat with the case of swords.

Captain Hutton then reclaimed the stage and, assisted by T.H. Toynbee, demonstrated a selection of Achille Marozzo's twenty-one methods by which an unarmed fighter could counter an attacker who was armed with a dagger. His selection was informed both by practicality and, he announced, by those which created "the most picturesque grouping of figures in stage performance." He followed this theme by demonstrating how smallsword fencers would make use of various disarming techniques, as he had alluded to in his lecture.

According to a reviewer from *The Stage* newspaper:

> "The two performances given by Miss Esme Beringer and Mr. George Silver were marked by a keenness and promptness of attack and defence that raised the enthusiasm of the spectators. Their first contribution was a very spirited engagement with rapier and dagger, in which Miss Beringer, though vanquished finally, revealed considerable skill and alacrity. Not less absorbing and stimulating was their encounter with dagger and cloak, in which some very smart play was witnessed, Mr. Silver scoring two points to one."

"Miss Beringer then invited the spectators to contribute to the discussion, and this appears to have been the cue for Egerton Castle to make his appearance on the stage. He confessed nothing but admiration for the technical skills that had been exhibited, but wanted to address the subject more strictly from the dramatic point of view. Noting that the finesse and detail of a stage fencing or wrestling match was apt to be lost, he made an appeal for consideration of fight sequences based on their psychological and emotional impact upon the play, noting that the simple act of drawing a sword on stage should resonate with dire import. Continuing in this vein, Castle asserted his opinion that the prolonged exchanges seen in many stage combats actually robbed those scenes of dramatic force, and therefore, that most stage fights should be short.

"Lady Colin Campbell, seated in the audience, was then invited to offer her comments, but she demurred with thanks, noting that her own experience of fencing was restricted to the modern forms of the art. The evening closed with a very warm vote of thanks to Miss Beringer for occupying the chair."

On the evening of March 12, Egerton Castle hosted a major fencing contest between French and Italian players at the Empress Rooms in Kensington. This event drew a great deal of popular and media attention as it was attended by King Edward. By this time, the Amateur Fencing Association was making great strides towards revitalizing the sport of fencing in England and the traditional rivalry between the French and Italian systems of fencing had become well known to the British sporting public.

Two days later, a production of the 1893 play *Saviolo*, by Castle and Walter Pollock, was performed at the Lyceum Theatre. Although it had been written for Henry Irving, and the theatrical impresario had bought an option on the script, he did not actually produce it formally at the Lyceum; this one-off production was for legal purposes, to secure copyright. Castle himself essayed the role of "Vincentio Saviolo," with Esme Beringer as "Edward Strange," her sister and fellow actress, Vera, as "Francesca," Guy Pollock as "Greene," C.H. Hughes as "Heronymo," James Brunton as "Strongitharm" and George Hayward as "Nicholl Harpeth."

On Tuesday July 15th, 1902, another exhibition of Elizabethan fencing was offered as part of an assault-at-arms in aid of the Charing Cross Hospital New Nurses' Home. The display began with a demonstration of military horsemanship and then a mass demonstration of the sword and lance drill (we may, perhaps, be forgiven for imagining Captain Hutton, who directed the ancient swordplay segment of the display, grinding his teeth during the soldier's sabre exercise).

According to a *London Times* review, the ancient swordplay commenced with Captain Stenson Cooke and Captain F.H. Whittow performing "a clever two-hand sword display, the fencing having been worked up from Marozza (sic), di Grassi and others." The second bout was described as a "Rapier and Dagger Duel under Henry III" and featured combat between two teams of three men each, as at the Albany Club exhibition several years previously. The Mignons were represented by Captain Hutton, A. Mansfield and Captain Stenson Cooke; the Guisards, by Lieutenant-Colonel Cyril Matthey, T.H. Toynbee and Captain Whittow. In this unusual bout, every fencer who received what he judged to be a valid "hit" fell as if dead, and when five of them were down, the victors bore away the weapons of the vanquished while black-hooded attendants entered to bear away the vanquished themselves.

The afternoon's diverse entertainment also included dramatic readings (by Esme Beringer, amongst others), a display of shadow pictures and a performance by the pipers of the 3rd Battalion Scots Guards.

On Wednesday, May 20th of the following year, Castle delivered a lecture on "Swordsmanship Considered Historically and as a Sport" for the Society of Arts. He began with an apology to the effect that, lacking the elbow-room he'd enjoyed on stage at the Lyceum Theatre twelve years previously, he would have to restrict himself to commentary rather than practical demonstration. He then acknowledged the influence of the article written by Sir Frederick Pollock, some twenty-one years earlier, and of Captain Hutton's contributions to the field.

This 1903 lecture, which was later published in article form, is especially interesting in that it reveals the evolution of Castle's opinions on the earlier forms of swordplay. His former, rather condescending attitude towards pre-16th-century swordsmanship seems to have mellowed, as had his assumption that the academic fencing of his own day necessarily represented the pinnacle of the art:

> "It may be stated from the outset that, although swordsmanship as a sport cannot yet be considered a popular one in England, although its adepts are few and none of them may be said to be of European reputation, nevertheless, it is in England beyond doubt that the true history of the art has been reconstructed.
>
> "... The oldest manuscript of fence belongs to Germany. It deals with the method of carrying out a wager of battle and the tricks of fight recommendable therefor. And pretty gruesome they are as a rule! I refer to Thalhofer's Fecht-Buch. The oldest printed book is likewise German: *Ergundung der ritterlicher Kunst der Fechterei, von Andreas Paurnfeindt, Freifechter zu Wien,* 1516. This work, which is exceedingly rare, is a very complete exponent of the ways of using long and short swords to the utmost of their lethal capacity—and quite irrespective of any sense of mere decorum.
>
> "... It is about this time, namely, the latter half of the 16th century, that we must take up our consideration of the development of sword-play pure and simple, for then a great change is perceptible in the nature and tendency of fence books: they approximate more and more to the consideration of what we now understand by fencing. The older works expounded the art of fight generally, taught the reader a number of valuable, if not always gentlemanly, dodges for overcoming an adversary at all manner of weapons: now the lucubrations of fence-masters during the last quarter of the 16th century deal almost exclusively with the walking sword, that is the duelling weapon: the rapier in fact, both with or without its lieutenant, the dagger."

Despite the fact that subsequent editions of *Schools and Masters of Fence* had retained most of the questionable assertions of the original, Castle's comments and tone in this lecture indicate that he had considerably modified his position. I suggest that there are three likely reasons why Castle's views on this subject might have changed significantly over the intervening nineteen years.

Firstly, there would have been the continued influence of his longtime friend, Alfred Hutton, who had always maintained a pragmatic interest in the sword as a fighting weapon, as distinct from a purely academic or sporting implement. As we have seen, Hutton had also become increasingly intrigued by close-combat techniques over the preceding several years.

Secondly, Castle had evidently been impressed by earlier combat treatises portraying systematic armoured fencing with the two-handed sword. His mention of Paurnfeindt's *Ergundung der ritterlicher Kunst der Fechterei* may be significant, in that this work does demonstrate a large degree of what Castle might have come to acknowledge as "scientific" theory and pedagogy. Depending on which of Talhoffer's several treatises Castle had perused during his research for *Schools and Masters,* he might be forgiven for not having perceived the science behind the use of the two-handed sword.

Thirdly, as was suggested earlier, when he wrote *Schools and Masters of Fence* Egerton Castle had been a twenty-six year old prodigy, burning with an ambition to establish himself as a writer and as an authority on the history of fencing. Entering middle age with his bona fides in both fields beyond reproach, he may simply have been better able to appreciate the history of fencing in less chauvinistic and more purely pragmatic terms.

A couple of months after Castle's lecture, Alfred Hutton returned to the London stage, choreographing the duel, or rather non-duel, for William Poel's production of Shakespeare's *Twelfth Night* at the Royal Court theatre. Shortly thereafter he performed an exhibition of "Tudor Sword-Play" at Cambridge University, with the assistance of Mr. T.H. Toynbee. The occasion was the revival of a play, first performed at Cambridge some three hundred years earlier, entitled *Worke for Cutlers, or, a Merry Dialogue betweene Sword, Rapier and Dagger.*" The script had been re-discovered and analyzed and the play re-mounted by the remarkable Albert Forbes Sieveking, who was to maintain something of an interest in fencing throughout his distinguished academic career. Mr. Sieveking made a strong case for the anonymous *Worke for Cutlers* having been written by the famed Jacobean playwright, Thomas Heywood.

Two years later, on Thursday, January 7th, 1904, Mr. Sieveking re-staged the play and again enlisted the help of T.H. Toynbee, but the 1904 production was not graced with Captain Hutton's presence. His longtime student and colleague, Cyril Matthey, substituted for the old Captain, performing, according to the program, a series of demonstrations with the broadsword and buckler opposed to broadsword and dagger after George Silver, the case of rapiers (i.e., fencing with one rapier in each hand) after Vincentio Saviolo, and finishing with an exhibition of rapier and dagger fencing. Curiously, despite what is asserted on the program, Saviolo's system did not actually address the case of rapiers. It seems safe to assume that Cyril Matthey would have known that very well, and so to attribute the mistake to a printing error.

Mr. Toynbee then assisted Captain Hutton in staging the swordplay for a production of *Romeo and Juliet* at the Court Theatre, premiering on the evening of Wednesday, February 17th. Their fight choreography was approvingly described as being "zealous."

On February 25th of 1904, Hutton offered an unusual presentation to the members of the Guthrie Society at Westminster Hospital:

> "Captain Alfred Hutton, the well-known fencer and author of *The Sword and the Centuries,* gave a demonstration of the methods of dealing with violent and refractory patients. The chairman pointed out that many medical men, especially those engaged in lunacy practice, were subject to attack by dangerous and irresponsible patients, whom it was desirable to disarm without inflicting on them bodily injury. The subject was not systematically taught in the (medical) schools, and every man had, on the spur of the moment, to act on his own initiative.
>
> "There were certain recognised methods of procedure in such cases, some of which were of Japanese origin, and there was no one in this country who had a larger experience of

> them than Captain Hutton. Yukio Tani's locks, various knock-out blows, the forcible removal of resisting people, and other methods were demonstrated on members of the Society, and the proceedings concluded with a vote of thanks to lecturer. It is probable that this new departure in the field of physical instruction will be followed by other medical schools."
>
> – *Medical Press and Circular,* Volume 128, 1904

Given both Hutton's long enthusiasm for George Silver's "gryps and clozes" and Achille Marozzo's *prese,* and the affinity between these European forms of close combat and jiujitsu, this report further demonstrates that Hutton had learned at least the basics of Japanese wrestling during his time at the Bartitsu Club. It's likely that this lecture/demonstration marks the first time an Asian martial art was specifically applied to the problems of humane self-defence and restraint in a European therapeutic setting.

Hutton's exhibition does, however, have a curious precedent in a self-defence and restraint system that was said to have been developed by workers in American psychiatric "asylums" during the mid-late 19th century. As described by Dr. Edward Huntingdon Williams in his book *The Walled City: a story of the criminal insane* (1913), this system, retroactively dubbed "American jiu jitsu," comprised some dozen escort holds and pressure-point control grips, covertly developed in response to the rule against psychiatric workers striking aggressive patients.

On Monday, May the 9th of 1904 Egerton Castle spoke to the Camera Club of the Society of Arts on *The Romance of Swordsmanship,* a lecture that combined his love of historical fencing with his imagination as a successful author of adventure fiction.

In a sense, these two latter presentations are emblematic of the natures of both men; though united by their abiding interest in ancient swordplay, their indefatigable promotion of competitive fencing and their long-standing friendship, Hutton was of an essentially pragmatic frame of mind, whereas Castle was a confirmed romantic. In that same sense, they were perhaps the ideal team to have initiated the revival of historical fencing in their day.

In his intriguing article *The Passing of the Duel* (Chambers's Magazine, 1906), Alfred Fellows speculated about the invention of a new and more civilised form of duelling, especially designed for English gentlemen. If properly overseen by a "Court of Honour," he argued, this would be a more manly and visceral form of redress than was allowed under the law in 1906.

> "(...) a duel with deadly weapons would be out of the question as a proper solution; and the aim being to punish the offender, such a thing as a fight with fists would be almost as undesirable, for as often as not the injured party would be thrashed. A possible solution would be to order the offender to be trounced up and flogged by the other, or otherwise arrange matters so that no harm could befall the innocent person; but apart from the fact that the guilty would never voluntarily submit to a tribunal which could only punish him, most gentlemen would feel that to hit a helpless man in cold blood was worse than receiving money from him as a solace for dishonour.
>
> "The problem is to find something which could be recognised as satisfactory by gentlemen, could take place in a school of arms or similarly suitable place, would not endanger life, would be capable of adjustment according to the righteousness of the respective causes, and perhaps having regard to size and reach (skill ought not to be so discounted), and would yet be an ordeal to both parties: the facing of sharp, physical pain, and the necessity of ignoring it. If it may be permitted to let imagination run riot for a minute, and to take unwarrantable liberties, a committee might be selected to consider the matter, and the services of Professor Sandow, Captain Alfred Hutton, Mr Eustace Miles, Mr Fry, and a professional boxer be commandeered, with some capable doctor to assist them. Perhaps, also, some professor of jiu jitsu would be useful, and these distinguished persons could then safely be left to devise a new and improved 'battel.'"

Given Hutton's sentiments on this subject, it's likely that he would have leapt at the chance to be involved in such a project if it had been proposed in earnest. For E.W. Barton-Wright's part, although may never have considered Bartitsu as a revival of the *code duello,* he would have appreciated, if not savored, the irony of Fellows' imagining a "new and improved 'battel'" for gentlemen combining boxing, physical culture, jiujitsu and Hutton's fencing, just four years after the closure of the Bartitsu Club.

The elderly Captain Hutton was evidently still keen on theatre. In November of 1907 he staged the sword fights for an otherwise ill-reviewed play entitled *1588,* a historical comedy in one act, and on March the 14th of 1908 premiered a new production of *Romeo and Juliet* at the Lyceum, for which Hutton's fight scenes were praised as "splendid" and "among the best ever seen."

Likewise, Egerton Castle was still very active as a fencing adjudicator, organizer of tournaments and even as a competitor. At the age of fifty, he captained the British Olympic fencing team in epee and sabre during the 1908 Olympiad.

During the same year, Egerton and Agnes Castle produced two short stories that returned to their familiar theme of fencing and dueling. The first, *My Rapier and My Daughter* was set in the year 1595, the plot broadly following that of Castle's play *Saviolo*:

> "Saviolo was fain to turn half aside to hide an irrepressible smile."I'll swear," was the thought singing joyously in his heart, 'I've not met a truer knight in all honourable England, nor a more valourous. Ay, he who would beard Saviolo himself in his den, and face his rapier for a woman's sake, is almost worthy of Saviolo's daughter. ... Sweet poet and sturdy fighter ... he belieth not his fame!'
>
> "'A noble flow of words, indeed,' he said, aloud, and feigning coldness. 'Art a most brave youth ... in words!'
>
> "'No more!' cried Strange, making the air hiss with his menacing blade. 'Draw, sir, or even now I strike!'

"Saviolo, pleased to his fill, stepped to the table, took up his rapier, and released it with leisurely grace. Then, balancing his dagger in his left hand, he fell on guard and smilingly received the reckless onslaught.

"But, although he smiled, never in his life had he fenced with more intent watchfulness or more closely brought his experience to bear upon his science. His slender double-edged blade was, towards the point, keen as a surgeon's knife: let but one unlucky stroke meet the lad on his headlong attacks and it might even cut the thread of Francesca's coming happiness. Ay, he would spare this gallant's blood—ay, even for its own sake. Yet it was imperative (so Saviolo thought) that this suitor should find out the worth of Saviolo's rapier, even as he had discovered that of Saviolo's daughter.

"'Methinks,' said the peerless swordsman, 'I mind me now thou hast a very homely scorn for the new-fangle rapier and its apish tricks. Despite all, shalt take lesson of Saviolo.' Here with his dagger he parried a furious lunge; then, with equal ease, took a murderous cut upon his hilt. 'Now, about those silken points of thine—it offends mine eye to see thee partly shorn. 'Twere neater to have none, or so it seems to me.'

"And, nimbly traversing right and left in front of his opponent, with the extreme edge of his blade he severed in quick succession the remaining points on the disordered doublet.

"'These twain upon thy sleeve,' he went on, bantering, 'they have a lonely look!'

"Now he evaded another stroke by the most unexpected incartade which placed him on his adversary's flank; and, upon the instant, sliced off yet another ribbon.

"By this time Strange was beside himself with rage. The skill which could have traversed his body a score of times or more, which could have slashed his face and hands, was yet nothing to the skill which thus spared, yet left its scornful mark at every stroke and in touches as delicate as a lady's scissors.

Better to lie weltering in blood than to be played with thus, defeated and yet protected!

"'Draw blood, Saviolo! ... Wound, kill!' he panted, 'but leave these devil's pranks!'

"Upon this cry he bounded like a panther—and would instantly have been impaled upon the despised foreign steel had not the master mercifully raised his point and contented himself with receiving on the joint blades of crossed rapier and dagger the cut that was meant to cleave him to the chine.

"Then, in a trice, followed one of Saviolo's most precious 'inclosings,' the secret of which was imparted only in the inner sanctum and belonged not to the practice-room. Rapier and dagger were dropped, clattering, on the floor; but, in the same second, the youth found himself disarmed and helpless, his own weapon, he knew not how, in his adversary's hand and its edge resting, thin and cold, on his own throat.

"But, far from carrying the lesson to its grim conclusion, Master Vincent gave the young man a good-natured push which sent him reeling back; then stood smiling (not without a little malicious complacency) upon the unwilling pupil, who, breathless, tore at his breast in futile despair.

" 'Thus it is done!' said Saviolo's voice."

– Egerton Castle and Agnes Castle,
My Rapier and My Daughter, 1908

The second story, *The Great Todescan's Secret Thrust*, appeared in the anthology *The Flower o' the Orange*. Undoubtedly Castle's *piece de resistence* of swashbuckling fiction, it was a romantic melodrama set entirely in the mileau of early 17th-century swordsmanship. The plot centers on one Dick Wyatt, a young English rapierist and former student of Saviolo's, and his quest to learn the *botte secrete* of an almost superhumanly skilled master known only as "the Todescan." There ensues a very great deal of fencing intrigue and the dropping of names from Carranza and Thibault to Meyer and Capoferro, interspersed with much swordplay, both in practice and in deadly earnest.

In its almost incantatory celebration of esoteric martial lore, *The Great Todescan's Secret Thrust* reads like nothing so much as a kung fu coming-of-age/revenge drama transplanted to Geneva in 1602.

> "Eh, la! Point in line, *figlio mio;* ever in line! And ever lower than the wrist! Lower, lower, good lad! Thumb down, and up with the little finger, elbow out, nearly straight! So, stand thus, and I promise thee ne'er a blade in the world shall surprise thy ward!"
>
> "As if in obedience, Dick swiftly fell into the well-known expectant guard. Even as he did so, there was a jerk—it was almost like an exclamation of wonder and disappointment—in the steel that pressed on his own; and Dick Wyatt was back again, fighting for his life, the Genevan cobblestones under his feet, the glimmer of the quick-match and its steady hiss, frightful menace warning him to haste! He gripped the ground in his soft shoes (a blessing it was, thought he swiftly, he had not waited to don the great boots!); he set his teeth. Never, for smallest breathing-space, did the Provost's terrible long blade release his own. He felt it gliding, seeking to bind, fiercely caressing; felt the deadly spring behind a tiger's crouch; felt the invincible, unknown thrust ready against his first weakening. And that weakening was coming apace! It was all he could do to hold his opposition. As a kind of spell cast by the fingers of steel, by the superhuman flexibility of his opponent's wrist, a palsy seemed to be creeping up his own outstretched arm. One twitch of relaxation, he knew, and he was sped!
>
> "Now, whether from the depth of his own need, or whether the spirit of the master were hovering over a beloved scholar in his dire extremity—who shall say?—certain it was that the very tones of Saviolo were now recalling to Wyatt's brain a favourite axiom of the fence-school:—
>
> "'Chi para, busca ... chi tira, tocca! ... He who parries but seeks ... he who thrusts, reaches!'

"It was to the youth as if a flame had been lit in his soul. Why wait in anguish to parry a coming secret thrust, when he could still himself strike? Up he sprang, brain and eye, wrist and nimble feet, in magnificent concert. To his dying day, Dick swore that, for the instant, he saw in the dark, even to the dreadful grin on the face opposite to him. His ear, strained to the same marvel of keenness, caught the sound of a catching breath—not his own. Exultant, he thrust; out went Saviolo's favourite botta lunga sopramano with point reverse!"

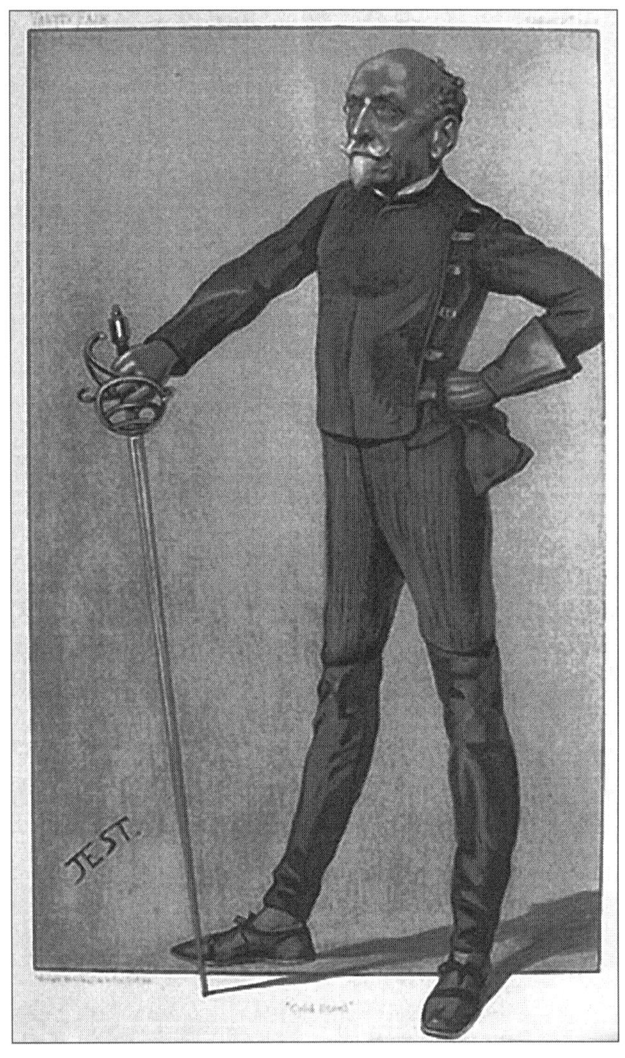

"Cold Steel" – Captain Alfred Hutton's caricature in *Vanity Faire* magazine (1903).

Chapter 12

Last of the Old Swordsmen (1910–20)

Captain Alfred Hutton died on December 18th, 1910, at the age of seventy-one.

An obituary written by his young colleague, A. Forbes Sieveking, described Hutton in these terms:

> "Of tall and picturesque figure, handsome face and chivalrous bearing, traits suggestive to friends of Don Quixote, he was wholehearted in his devotion to the science of arms, which he did much to rescue from neglect."

Hutton was buried in Astbury Churchyard, Cheshire and a memorial tablet was unveiled by his nephew, Lieutenant-General Sir Edward Hutton, on October 8th, 1911. His friend Colonel Cyril Matthey was one of the executors of his last will and testament, and Captain Hutton's fine collection of fencing books, arms and armour was bequeathed to the Victoria and Albert museum. The museum library presently houses Hutton's collection of 371 books in 391 volumes dealing with fencing and combat sports, including wrestling and boxing, of the 16th to 19th centuries. Further collections of books formerly owned by Alfred Hutton are in the Corble Collection, located at the Universiteitsbibliotheek at the Katholieke Universiteit te Leuven and the Emil Fick Library, located at the Livrustkammaren (Sweden).

With Hutton's passing, much of the verve seems to have passed from the "ancient swordplay" movement in England.

On Thursday, June 13th of 1912, Egerton Castle hosted a semi-theatrical exhibition of historical fencing in aid of the Actors' Benevolent Fund. Sir George Alexander donated the use of St James's Theatre for the presentation, which featured skits written by some of the top London playwrights of the day framing a series of combat demonstrations, presented in tongue-in-cheek fashion as a "Movement to Revive Dueling." These skits were performed by members of the recently-founded Actors' Sword Club and by a number of noted amateur fencers, but only Cyril Matthey is listed as a representative of the original London Rifle Brigade/Bartitsu Club eras. Ernest Stenson Cooke was not available, as he was representing England in fencing at the Olympic Games in Stockholm, Sweden.

After this successful event, Egerton Castle appears to have largely retired from the world of historical fencing. War was approaching and, as Castle entered his twilight years, his beloved romance must have seemed to be fast fading from the world.

Castle died on September 19th, 1920. His obituary in the *National Register* of that year read:

> "Egerton Castle, M.A., F.S.A., was born in 1858, and was educated at the Universities of Paris and Glasgow, and graduated from Trinity College, Cambridge, in the Natural Science Tripos. He passed through Sandhurst, and the Inner Temple, and eventually became chairman of the company which bore the name of his grandfather, the founder of the Liverpool Mercury, which was subsequently amalgamated with the Daily Post. Mr. Castle was a fine rifle and pistol shot, and a famous swordsman. He held for many years the amateur championship of Great Britain, resigning the title unbeaten, and he was Captain of the British epee and sabre teams at the Olympic Games in 1908. He also became Captain in the Royal Engineers Militia (Portsmouth Division, Submarine Miners).

"Mr. Castle began to write at the age of 26, when he published *Schools and Masters of Fence*. He worked on the staff of the Saturday Review, published a novel, *Consequences*, in 1891, which he followed up by a work on *English Book Plates*, a play for Sir Henry Irving, and a translation into French of Stevenson's *Prince Otto*. The long series of romantic novels in which Mr. Castle collaborated with his wife brought to both of them a great popular reputation. From 1898, when they published *The Pride of Jennico*, every year saw the production of one of their charming romances, several of which were dramatized, and in *The Hope of the House*, which appeared in 1915, the authors showed a greater depth and power than had been apparent before the war. Mr. Castle was survived by his wife and daughter."

Agnes Castle lived for two more years.

With the passing of Egerton Castle, we really come to the end of the "ancient swordplay" story, for the time being. I have been unable to find any references to a continuation of classes, demonstrations, books or lectures in the old Hutton/Castle tradition after Egerton Castle's participation in the 1912 display at St. James's Theatre.

This rather begs the question of "what happened next?" After so much time, thought, and energy had been put into reviving historical fencing from the early 1880s, how is it that the subject was then so thoroughly forgotten during the first half of the 20th century?

Although the creation of the Olympic Games would guarantee the survival of modern fencing in England, the move towards a standardized curriculum left little place for training with antique weapons.

Chapter 13

Whither, Ancient Swordplay?

In assessing the apparent failure of the ancient swordplay revival to flourish in England during the post-Edwardian era, we must first consider the motivations of the revivalists.

It is obvious that the intrinsic intellectual fascination of discovering and studying old treatises, as well as the technical challenges of deciphering their instructions, were enough to sustain both Alfred Hutton and Egerton Castle. Both men were kernoozers in the truest sense. However, and crucially for present purposes, we should recall that Hutton and Castle were also working very hard to secure the survival of fencing itself in their homeland, as a sport and as a gentlemanly accomplishment.

During the 1880s their greatest hurdle had been the fact that fencing, per se, was simply not a popular activity among English athletes. As Captain Hutton had frequently complained, it was very seldom taught in schools or colleges. Various contemporary writers proposed different reasons for this state of affairs, including the pragmatic reality that, as dueling had long-since fallen out of fashion, the use of the sword had become obsolete as a means of civilian self-defence; several suggested that it had effectively been replaced by boxing. The frequent speculations in the popular press regarding a revival of dueling in England had almost always been facetious; the notion of settling affairs of honor with cold steel was abhorrent to the progressive zeitgeist of English society at the turn of the 20th century.

Most commentators agreed that the sport of fencing was also widely considered to be somehow "un-English." The late 19th century was the height of European colonialism and was a time of intense nationalism; the impression of a given activity as being "not the done thing," or, even worse given the traditional rivalries, as being "Frenchified," was a daunting cultural barrier against any attempt at popular success.

This was also a period of intense class-consciousness. By the 1890s, as many sports were becoming better organized at the local and national levels, they grew to depend on the burgeoning middle classes for their continued prosperity. Throughout most of the preceding century, though, fencing in England had been associated primarily with the aristocracy. Comparable to foxhunting and mountaineering, it had very little in the way of support at the grass-roots level.

While there were several well-regarded *salles d'armes* in England, mostly located in London, they had traditionally catered to a comparatively small, wealthy and socially elite clientele. Prior to the establishment of the Amateur Fencing Association, the sport had offered only sporadic activity at the civilian inter-club competitive level and had possessed very little in the way of an administrative infrastructure.

As Hutton had said in *Old Sword Play*, however, with reference to the utility of studying historical styles, "everything ... is useful to the Art of Fence which tends to create an interest in it." Thus, a significant part of the Hutton/Castle agenda in staging exhibitions of ancient swordplay was to encourage a wider interest in the contemporary, internationally competitive systems of fencing. In his *English Masters of Arms* (1956), fencing historian J.D. Aylward referred to their efforts as a successful "campaign of propaganda." Given the sentimental climate of the day, that agenda also, undoubtedly, included re-contextualizing fencing as a proud English tradition.

Through their exhibitions, very often in aid of various charities, as well as through their lectures, books and articles, Castle and Hutton had fostered not only an appreciation of the history of swordsmanship, but also a general enthusiasm for fencing that resulted in stronger organization and increased competitive activity in foil, sabre and eventually epee at the club level. Hutton, in particular, also frequently took the opportunity to politicise his ancient swordplay exhibitions by addressing his audiences on the state of military close combat training.

These were politically sophisticated men who must have realized that, in attempting to promote the contemporary sport of fencing in England, they were starting well behind the pack. They were acutely aware of the fact that swordplay had never faded from fashion on the European continent and that they had their work cut out for them in cultivating English fencers who could realistically hope to challenge their French and Italian contemporaries. However, as Castle had pointed out in introducing his 1903 lecture for the Society of Arts:

> "It may be stated from the outset that, although swordsmanship as a sport cannot yet be considered a popular one in England, although its adepts are few and none of them may be said to be of European reputation, nevertheless, it is in England beyond doubt that the true history of the art has been reconstructed."

Simultaneously with its promotional value in reintroducing modern fencing to their countrymen, their eccentric and colorful specialization of ancient swordplay also offered an area in which English fencers could establish themselves internationally, and even take the lead, as was borne out when Castle was elected to the Academie d'Armes and when Hutton and his students were invited to demonstrate their skills in Brussels.

Thus, through their promotional efforts, their organization of tournaments and, most especially, their tireless efforts on behalf of the Amateur Fencing Association, Hutton and Castle had unquestionably succeeded in fostering an infrastructure that supported the revival of amateur fencing in England. The same, evidently, could not be said for their revival of ancient swordplay, which was for most intents and purposes forgotten after the First World War; however, there is little evidence to suggest that they ever actually intended for that revival to outlive them. I would argue that by the time Hutton had passed on in 1910, their revival of ancient swordplay had largely fulfilled its intended functions.

Egerton Castle does not appear to have taken an active role in teaching these skills, other than by coaching actors for stage roles; thus, it remains for us to look towards Captain Hutton's students. These are the fencers who, under other circumstances, might have comprised the second generation of ancient swordplay instructors in England; Cyril Matthey, in particular, seeming the most likely heir apparent to Hutton's historical fencing legacy.

It is certain that Castle, Hutton, and Matthey were among the best English representatives of historical fencing styles during the late 19th century. Given their long-term training with Hutton at the London Rifle Brigade School of Arms and the Bartitsu Club, and their participation in multiple historical fencing events throughout the 1890s, it is evident that Carl Thimm, Ernest Stenson Cooke, E.D. Johnson, W.P. Gate and Frank H. Whittow could also have given good accounts of themselves.

Sir Frederick and Walter Herries Pollock are "wild cards." While the brothers were evidently avid fencers, with Sir Frederick, in particular, taking an early and serious interest in the history of swordplay, we have only a few references to either of them having taken an active part in historical fencing events. Likewise, whereas the athletic William Henry Grenfell (Lord Desborough) fenced with Hutton at rapier and daggers for the Bath Club display in 1899, and continued as an active fencer for decades afterwards, he seems to have played no further role in the revivalist effort. Nor does Sir Guy Laking, who participated in the 1901 exhibition for the Society of Antiquaries, appear to have taken any further active part in the "ancient fencing" movement.

Many others—Mssrs. Rolt, Harvey, Collard, Toynbee, Buzzard, Marillier, Harvest, H.A. Dunn, Blackburn et al—are known to us only through their participation in one or two of Hutton's exhibitions.

This line of speculation is further complicated by the fact that an individual's participation in a historical fencing display does not necessarily indicate prolonged, thorough training in the art. For example, an experienced and confident athlete who was also an epeeist, bayonetist and/or sabreur might have agreed to take part in such a display for fun or as a favour, and simply played the role of the "fall guy" in set-play demonstrations, and relied upon improvisation, rather than historical precedent, if called upon to bout.

According to Eleanor Baldwin Cass, the author of *The Book of Fencing* (1930), fencer and fencing bibliophile Achibald H. Corble:

> "... always specialized in sabre fencing, but was also interested in the early forms of swordplay, such as rapier-and-dagger, double-hander, and sword-and-buckler, having been a pupil of the late Captain Alfred Hutton, the great authority and writer on the subject. (Corble) has organized and taken part in numerous displays of modern and ancient fencing, notably those entitled 'The Duel Throughout the Ages' held at the Botanical Gardens, and one given at the St. James Theatre in 1912, arranged by the late Egerton Castle."

As Corble had started fencing in 1901, he probably studied under Hutton at the Bartitsu Club, and if so, would likely have been among Hutton's last students of ancient swordplay.

It appears that of the men who are known to have made an active study of ancient swordplay with Alfred Hutton, only Corble, Grenfell, Stenson Cooke and Gate were still active in amateur fencing during the first decades of the 20th century. We can only assume that they lacked the motivation to maintain, or to revive, the work begun by Hutton and Egerton Castle. Perhaps they felt that, as competitive foil, epee and sabre fencing had by then become well-established, there was no need to continue to stage exhibitions of the historical styles; their sentiment may have been that ancient swordplay had already served its major purpose of fostering enthusiasm for the contemporary fencing sports.

The enormous psychological and physical toll taken by the First World War must also have played a part. There seems little doubt that some of the young men who had trained with Hutton perished in the trenches, although Cyril Matthey, who was certainly the most senior and active of Hutton's disciples, survived his tour of duty in France with the London Rifle Brigade. It is possible that in the after the death of Captain Hutton and into the post-War years, the continued pursuit of antique fencing was simply deemed to be naïvely, or even painfully, nostalgic by the few men for whom it would have been practical.

The homogenizing effect of the modern Olympic Games must also have contributed towards the decline of ancient swordplay. Whereas a member of a London salle d'armes during the late 19th century might have learned to fence with the bayonet, quarterstaff and other weapons, only the three "modern" fencing sports were selected for the Olympic Games after 1900. An exception occurred at the 1904 Games in St. Louis, Missouri, USA, which also included a singlestick tournament.

As the Olympics grew in stature throughout the early 1900s, much pressure was placed upon national sporting societies and, therefore, upon local clubs as well, to focus on the "official" Olympic codes. In the rush of modernization that characterized the post-War years and carried through into the 1920s, training in antique fencing styles may have seemed less of a romantic diversion and more of a pointless anachronism.

The next avenue to consider is that of ancient swordplay itself as a competitive sport. The organization of inter-club fencing tournaments during the 1880s and, increasingly, during the '90s, had fostered a strong foundation consolidated under the auspices of the Amateur Fencing Association from 1902 onwards. Although Captain Hutton had formulated rules for various, more orthodox, forms of fencing, including a comprehensive "generic" rule-set, he does not appear to have published rules for bouting with rapier and dagger, sword and buckler, etc. beyond those implied by his selection of source material for *Old Swordplay* in 1892. Nor are there any records of Hutton having promoted competitions in these styles other than bouting displays in his numerous historical fencing exhibitions. This further suggests that fostering the actual practice of ancient swordplay outside of his circle of colleagues was not among his priorities. If it had been, then the challenge of regular competition, in tandem with foil, epee and sabre contests, might have spurred a larger and more enduring revivalist effort. As we shall see, this direction was later taken by others.

Aside from its use in promoting fencing as a whole and (potentially) as a sport in its own right, ancient swordplay might have found some practical application in military training. Curiously, there appears to be no indication that the practice of historical fencing was continued at the School of Arms of the London Rifle Brigade, nor the King's Dragoon Guards, despite their long association with Captain Hutton. Likewise, as was mentioned previously, the British Army never adopted the proposals by Hutton and Matthey for a form of simplified, combat-oriented sabre fighting influenced by the "gryps" of George Silver. Despite the vehement arguments on both sides of that controversy during the 1890s, it was soon to become moot. After the First World War, military swordsmanship was increasingly relegated to ceremony and sport, in favour of a stripped-down system of close-combat instruction with the rifle-bayonet for actual combat.

The Kernoozers Club, which had once hosted Egerton Castle's private exhibitions of historical fencing and which might have maintained the tradition into the early 20th century, finally disbanded in 1922. However, the Meyrick Society, which was originally founded as a breakaway faction known as the Junior Kernoozers, is still active today.

The final theme to consider is that of the influence of ancient swordplay upon the practice of stage combat. As we have seen, both Alfred Hutton and Egerton Castle were theatre aficionados and also experienced fight directors. Other than soldiers, actors were among the only people who had any professional use for swordplay, and most particularly, for archaic styles such as the use of the broadsword and handbuckler or rapier and dagger.

An American fencer named Fred Gilbert Blakeslee had both studied the books written by Hutton and Castle and also corresponded with both men. Formerly the Swordmaster of the Connecticut National Guard, Blakeslee took an avid interest in historical fencing and contributed a number of articles on that subject to various American periodicals during the first decade of the 20th century. In 1905 Blakeslee wrote a book, *Sword-Play for Actors,* detailing his system for adapting both historical and academic/sporting styles of fencing for stage combat, and he also worked as a fight director and stage combat instructor. For all of Blakeslee's evident enthusiasm, though, it appears that his efforts to continue the historical fencing revival in the USA did not bear any lasting fruit.

However, Castle and Hutton did have some enduring impact upon the enactment of Shakespeare's duels and battles on the London stage. Prior to their engagements as fight directors during the 1890s and Hutton's classes for actors at the Bartitsu Club in the early 1900s, scant heed had been taken of the idea of historical accuracy in either stage weaponry or fighting styles. Afterwards, it became increasingly common for theatrical duels to be fought with historically appropriate prop weapons.

The detail of whether their fight choreography, based directly upon the fencing of George Silver and other old masters, may have been absorbed into the general body of stage practice in London during the early 1900s has, unfortunately, been lost. However, in his 1902 lecture for the Playgoers' Club, Hutton had expressed his hopes that the younger generation of actors would continue to "improve stage fighting," by which he obviously meant that they should continue to represent historically accurate fighting styles on stage.

It is notable that the Actresses' Foil Club—originally the "ladies' branch" of the Actors' Sword Club, whose members had participated in Egerton Castle's last recorded ancient swordplay exhibition in 1912—included Esme Beringer among its members. While the Actors' Sword Club was suspended during World War One, the women's club was sustained during that period and may represent a survival of the teachings of Hutton and Castle into the 1920s and, possibly, beyond.

As we have seen, Esme Beringer was an active and enthusiastic student of both Hutton's and Castle's at the height of their activities as exhibitors of ancient swordplay. In a 1903 interview, Miss Beringer recalled that:

> "... Mr. Egerton Castle was not my first 'Saviolo' (fencing instructor). When (my sisters and I) were quite little at home we had a fencing master, Sergeant Elliott. That, I suppose, was when I first learned to love fencing. After that I left it alone for a time, but my early tuition came in useful years afterward when Captain Hutton very kindly and generously offered to prepare me for *Romeo and Juliet*, which was produced at the Prince of Wales.'
>
> "His knowledge of the swordsmanship of the period, as well as his instruction, were invaluable. My next experience of fencing on the stage was with Mr. Castle in a fencing dialogue he had written round Saviolo and his pupil Luke—a little piece which we first played at Mr. George Alexander's big bazaar at the Great Central Hotel.
>
> "Subsequently we repeated the performance at Bertrand's, and this led to my Palace engagement when my brother George Silver appeared with me in *At the Point of the Sword*. During

our engagement at the Palace we were asked to appear in a piece on behalf of the Actor's Benevolent Fund, which we did, as also later at Drury Lane, the Lyceum and the Alhambra, at Bristol, Brighton and Oxford. Then I must not forget that I had the honour of taking the chair at Capt. Hutton's interesting lecture at the Playgoer's Club on *Stage Fights*."

– Kaufman C. Spiers, "Fencing and the Stage," *The Playgoer*, Vol. III Nov. 1902–Apr. 1903

At the Point of the Sword evidently borrowed from Castle's *Saviolo*, although the playlet took the plot in a rather different direction:

"The scene is laid in the house of Savario, an Italian nobleman. Geoffrey, surnamed 'Swift o' the Steel,' a bold and daring youth, has wrongs to set right, and he takes advantage of a lesson in 'the deadly thrust' given him by his teacher, Savario, who is his adversary, to attack that gentleman and kill him. All were delighted by the grace and skillfulness of Miss Beringer's fencing, and her thrust and parry were declared excellent. Indeed, the trifle served to show how fine a swordswoman the talented actress is, and her cleverness in the play of rapier and dagger. Mr. Geo. Silver as Savario made a formidable foe to the dauntless 'Swift o' the Steel' and fought with consummate skill. The small part of Sebastian was well cared for by Mr. Pym Williamson. The sketch was well-staged, and will no doubt remain in the bill for some time to come."

– *The Stage*, September 12, 1901

Thus, Esme Beringer's participation in ancient swordplay exhibitions took three forms. As a professional actress she relished the chance to display her skills with the rapier and dagger in formal theatrical productions such as *Romeo and Juliet*. She was an enthusiastic participant in several of the lecture/demonstrations arranged by Castle and Hutton, even chairing one of those events for the prestigious Playgoers Club. During these presentations she took part in free-bouting as well as in set-play demonstrations. She also performed in theatrical sketches, short one-act plays whose purpose, in essence, was to justify a "terrific combat" between herself and her fellow actor and historical fencing enthusiast, George Silver.

Beringer later taught fencing to members of the Actresses' Franchise League, representing the cause of women's suffrage in the theatrical community, and as late as 1938 she was still exercising her fighting skills on the London stage, during an extraordinary performance in the title role of *Hamlet*. In Esme Beringer (1875–1972), we have at least one example of a member of the Hutton/Castle lineage who maintained aspects of their "ancient swordplay" into the mid-20th century.

Interestingly, there had been a short-lived revival of ancient swordplay displays, reminiscent of the old Hutton/Castle tradition, arranged for several Royal Tournaments during the early 1920s. These displays were performed by members of the Army Physical Training Corps, which had formerly been supervised by Colonel G. Malcolm Fox, Captain Hutton's nemesis in the Army fencing debate of the 1890s.

Contemporary reports are sketchy at best, but it is evident that these were semi-theatrical presentations, in keeping with the long Royal Tournament tradition of costumed historical re-enactments. The soldiers who performed in the *Duelling Displays* between 1922–25 wore representations of Renaissance-era clothing, including hoods worn over fencing masks, while bouting with rapier and dagger, sword and buckler and rapier and cloak. Their costume for quarterstaff fencing appears to have been almost identical to that worn by the original Army quarterstaff revivalists some fifty years earlier. Unfortunately, it is unknown as to whether there was any lineal connection between the APTC *Duelling Displays* of the '20s and the activities of the Hutton/Castle clique.

Finally, it is worth noting that British fight directors of the 1960s were more than tangentially aware of historical fencing treatises, partly via their relatively easy access to the books written by Hutton and Castle. Arthur Wise's book *Weapons in the Theatre* (1968) begins by quoting Sir Guy Laking and Egerton Castle (Kernoozers, both) on the subject of historical accuracy in stage fight choreography. Wise goes on to discuss historical masters including Saviolo and Silver, and the stage combat techniques put forth in his book draw a good deal of inspiration from historical sources, without any attempt at verbatim representation.

Thus, whereas the recreational practice of historical fencing as a form of "antagonistics"—what we would today refer to as a martial art—did not survive its second generation, it did continue to influence professional stage combat in England. In seeking out further survivals of the Hutton/Castle legacy of ancient swordplay, it remains for us to look towards France.

"L'Escrime a travers les Ages" – from the cover of *L'Illustration*, 1894.

Chapter 14

L'escrime a Travers les Ages (A Return to Monnaie, 1894)

As we have seen, Egerton Castle's exhibitions on the stage of the Lyceum Theatre in 1891 created a public awareness of, and curiosity about, the new pastime of "ancient swordplay." His coups had been to include some of his celebrated colleagues as performers, to secure the involvement and support of Henry Irving and, especially, to be asked to repeat the exhibition for Prince Edward. Thus, Castle achieved an aura of both moral and intellectual respectability for historical fencing that was several steps above the carnival atmosphere of the circus ring and the music hall stage. By making the attendance of such exhibitions fashionable for the educated classes at a time of pervasive class-consciousness, Castle established a precedent for the numerous similar presentations offered by himself and by Alfred Hutton in the following years.

It is highly likely that Castle's *Schools and Masters of Fence,* followed by the success of his Lyceum Theatre exhibitions a few years later, had inspired Albert Fierlants, the president of the Cercle d'Escrime in Brussels, to organize his own festival of the sword, which, as was previously mentioned, took place in 1894. Fierlants had been well aware of the recent developments in England, as he had been responsible for the (authorized) French translation of Castle's seminal work.

The chosen theme, *L'Escrime a Travers les Ages,* was suitably romantic, promising an exhibition of cultural and historical interest as well as fun and spectacle. The venue, the magnificent Royal Opera House in Monnaie, at least rivaled London's celebrated Lyceum Theatre in grandeur. Perhaps the fencers of the Cercle d'Escrime de Bruxelles were attempting to demonstrate, in deed as well as word, "anything the English can do, we can do better."

If so, it is ironic that while the Cercle d'Escrime had invited fencing clubs from throughout Belgium and France to send delegate/performers to Monnaie, the only participants from outside the Francophone world were Captain Alfred Hutton, Cyril Matthey, and some of their students from the School of Arms of the London Rifle Brigade.

Behind the scenes on the morning of Saturday, May 21, hundreds of fencers and supernumerary performers were donning their armour and costumes; the fencers then limbered up by rehearsing their fight routines. Teams of scene-shifters were checking the elaborate painted backdrops, representing an ancient Roman arena, a medieval tournament field, a forest clearing. Meanwhile, a large crowd milled outside the theatre, including many family groups, attracted by colorful posters and by newspaper advertisements that had promised an edifying spectacle, entertaining and educating in equal measure.

The exhibition consisted of ten combats representing different eras, and therefore fought with different weapons and fencing styles. Each fight sequence was contextualized with a short playlet, written specifically for the festival.

The most spectacular of these scenes was a "combat aux armes courtoisies" fought between actors portraying the knights Jacques de Lalain and Thomas Que. The famous old society of fencers, the Chef-Confrarie de Saint Michel de Gent, had leant a historic banner that adorned the pavilion of the actor representing their champion. There were at least two hundred performers on the stage during that scene alone.

The remaining scenes showcased combats fought with a range of weapons, including the case of rapiers, two-handed swords, rapiers and cloaks, etc., each fight framed within its own story.

The Monnaie exhibition was a smash success. Reviewers praised the "fidelity and exactness" with which the fencers had illustrated the fencing styles of "all schools and all eras." Special mention was made of the English fencers:

> "They are accustomed to handling ancient weapons, and their demonstration was a wonderful achievement, even in the eyes of an audience comprised largely of novices with regards the art and science of fencing. The combat in each scene, arising logically from the (dramatic) situation, was most impressive, as much in contests of armoured fighting with axes as in those fought with the two-handed sword, the sword and buckler, the rapier, etc.
>
> "The audience was also fascinated by the displays of intricate historical fencing drills, because of the interesting postures and the precision of movement in both attacking and defensive attitudes."
>
> – Gabriel Letainturier-Fradin,
> *La Theatre Heroique*, c.1912

Other than courtesy, it seems likely that the English fencers were singled out for special praise because they had actually spent a number of years training in the styles they were representing for the exhibition. Hutton later mentioned that his team from the L.R.B. School of Arms had been given the "leading fighting roles" in the festival, and the organisers were obviously impressed with their skills.

Although fencing with the canne (stick), baton (staff), epee, sabre and foil were widely practiced throughout France, and French antiquarians had produced histories and bibliographies of swordplay, I have not found any records of the active, scholarly reconstruction of historical fencing styles in that country prior to 1894.

In his preface to the 1896 edition of *A Complete Bibliography of Fencing and Duelling*, Carl Thimm wrote of the Monnaie exhibition:

> "Paradoxical as it may seem, help, both in information and in personnel, had to be sought from England.

> "(...) and (the Monnaie exhibition) derived its chief element of success from the presence and active help of Captain A. Hutton and several English officers of the Volunteers, his companions in arms, who went over to lend the weight of their special and remarkable dexterity."

In his book *Escrimeurs Contemporains* (1899), Henry de Goudourville offered a comprehensive series of biographies of notable fencers and fencing masters. His entry concerning Captain Alfred Hutton supports the contention that it was Hutton and his students who, in effect, introduced to France the practice of systematic historical accuracy in reconstructing ancient swordplay, via their performance at the Royal Monnaie Opera House:

> "(Hutton's) publication of a book entitled *Old Sword Play,* in 1892, inspired him to perpetuate, in a modern form, the picturesque systems of fencing of the XV, XVI and XVII centuries, with the Elizabethan rapier, etc. It is to him, also, that we owe the reconstitution of the old plays of the schools of the past, in which he excels and with which has such success in England. This book also caused him to be elected an official member of the Society of Antiquaries. It was undoubtedly the publication of this work that, in 1894, decided the late Albert Fierlants, then president of the Cercle d' Escrime of Brussels, to invite Captain Hutton to his 'Tournament of Fencing Through the Ages,' to which he was accompanied by Captain Matthey, Messrs. Cooke, Whittow, Gate and Johnson, representing the fencers of England.
>
> "Since then Captain Hutton's expertise has often been employed, as was that of the late Professor Bertrand, in the staging of duels in the theater.
>
> "(...) (Captain Hutton's swordsmanship) is noted especially for its romantic character, inspired by the old treatises that he so enjoys consulting, bringing to life the picturesque and decorative costumes and beautiful weapons of our ancestors."

In terms of the lineage of historical fencing, the greatest significance of the Monnaie exhibition may have been the exposure of hundreds of French fencers to the achievements of Hutton's small group from the School of Arms of the London Rifle Brigade.

By way of contrast with the situation in England during the early 1890s, fencing was a matter of established tradition and even of national pride in France. Duels of honour were still being fought clandestinely with the sabre and the epee, and there were dozens of fencing societies representing all orthodox branches of the discipline, from specialized military organizations to representative bodies for fencing in secondary schools and in private physical culture gymnasia. All of this activity required a strong fencing infrastructure, even amongst competing factions.

In both England and France, "ancient swordplay" was generally seen as an antiquarian eccentricity, or at its most practical, as a way to enliven assaults-at-arms and as a source of inspiration for stage combat. Thus, the great majority of fencers tended not to pursue that study as seriously as they did the more modern competitive, academic and dueling forms of the art. Still, and crucially for the purposes of our interests, the size and organization of the French fencing "establishment" provided a foundation that would ultimately allow versions of *escrime ancienne* to flourish beyond the lifetimes of individual enthusiasts.

So it was that the twilight years of English historical fencing marked the rise of a new French "star"; a remarkable athlete/artist named Georges Dubois who was, more than anyone else, responsible for keeping the torch aflame into the first decades of the 20th century.

Dubois' syncretic rapier and dagger fencing, from *L'Escrime au Theatre* (1910).

Chapter 15

The Artistic Archeaology of Vanished Fighting Arts: Georges Dubois and L'escrime Ancienne

Dubois was born in 1865. At the time of the Brussels exhibition he was twenty-nine years old and was gaining acclaim in the art world through his work as a professional sculptor, creating portrait busts and medallions of famous personalities as well as allegorical works including *Cet age est sans pitie* (1889), *Siecles future* (1891) and *Apres la faute* (1899). His masterpiece was considered to be a bust of Chopin, which he produced in 1910 and which was installed in the Jardin de Luxembourg.

Like Hutton and Castle, Dubois was both a creative intellectual and a serious physical culturist, with a particular passion for all forms of hand-to-hand combat. Classically handsome and powerfully built at 5' 7" and a little over 165 lbs, he had trained in boxing, la savate (French kickboxing) and fencing since childhood.

George Dubois represented France at the Olympic Games in 1900 (competing in an extremely grueling gymnastics event) and in 1905 he took part in an unusual jiujitsu versus French boxing challenge contest. This match was heavily promoted by and debated within the French sporting press for months beforehand. Dubois' opponent, Ernest Regnier (who went by the quasi-Japanese nom du guerre of Re-Nie), was a Parisian wrestler who had attracted the patronage of physical culture impresario Edmond Desbonnet. Desbonnet had sponsored Regnier's jiujitsu training in London, with former Bartitsu Club instructor Yukio Tani.

The savate vs. jiujitsu challenge bout wastreated almost as a formal duel of national honour, being attended by some 500 dignitaries and celebrities. The fight itself, however, was anti-climactic. After some preliminary sparring, Regnier parried Dubois' first kick and closed; the two men went to the ground and the savateur was almost immediately forced to submit to an extended arm-bar. The actual combat had lasted only 6 seconds. Chastened and impressed, Dubois went on to add elements of the Japanese art of self-defence to his own repertoire of skills.

By 1906, Dubois had become interested in the intellectual and physical challenges of reviving archaic systems of fence. His first project was the reconstruction of Roman gladiatorial combat between a *retiarius* (net and trident fighter) and a *myrmillo* (sword and shield fighter), to be demonstrated at an "ancient sports" festival in Tourcoing. As mentioned earlier, there was a long-standing French tradition of staging elaborate sporting fêtes in imitation of the classical Greek and Roman games. The modern international Olympiad is actually a survival of this tradition.

Unlike his English predecessors, Dubois thoroughly documented his process of reconstructing historical fighting arts in interviews and articles for magazines such as *La Culture Physique*, as is précised below.

Accepting that his reconstruction was necessarily going to be speculative, there being no surviving manuals of gladiatorial combat, Dubois' method was to first hire an armourer to construct functional replicas of the requisite weapons and armour, a process taking several months. As his armament was being assembled, he pored over classical images and descriptions of gladiatorial combat, trying to absorb the "psychology" of the fighters and their culture, which he felt to be very important.

Once the armour was ready for field-testing, Dubois and his associate, Morris del-Prat, began practical experiments based on the ergonomics of the weapons and armour themselves. The combination of co-operative drills and competitive sparring exercises enabled him to deduce the way in which certain fighting techniques would likely have been performed and then combined; an approach that his colleague Gabriel Letainturier-Fradin referred to as "the artistic archeaology of vanished fighting arts."

Dubois also devised nicknames for the various techniques that he developed. For example, the "sparrowhawk throw" was so-called because of the shape the net formed when it was swung and cast in a particular way, reminiscent of a bird of prey spreading its wings. When that technique failed to ensnare his opponent, Dubois noted that, in falling to the ground between the two fighters, the net created an obstacle for the myrmillo, who could not step on the net for fear of having his feet pulled out from underneath him.

If the retiarius then stepped back, the net was drawn into the shape of a spindle. Dubois then had the idea of using this "spindle" as a lashing weapon. He devised techniques for entangling the myrmillo's head, feet or sword. Another attack, which Dubois considered to be one of the most formidable, he named the "spindle and turn-up." Stepping back while dragging the net before him, he would then execute the retiarian equivalent of a stop-lunge with his left arm, suddenly casting the net upwards to entangle the weapon-bearing arm and the head of the myrmillo.

Dubois' reconstruction was praised in a detailed article published by *La Culture Physique* (1906):

> "The working process used by Mr. Dubois is notable due to its simplicity. Every athlete can assimilate it because, in short, it is all a matter of time and patience.
>
> "In Tourcoing, Mssrs. Georges Dubois and Morris del-Prat, who are both very nimble and formidable fencers, did a wonderful job in making gladiatorial fights accessible to the general public. M. Dubois, who played the retiarius, has discovered many movements allowing the use of the net, which is a difficult exercise, requiring agility, strength and extreme precision of movement, because it is necessary to control the net with your left hand while striking with the trident in your right hand. You must leap, pursue, feint or rush to escape, and also contend hand-to-hand. This style of fighting makes full use of the left side of the body, so often neglected in ordinary fencing drills.

"As for tactics, the two champions adopted the following theme in their demonstrations: to allow the initial net attacks to fall short, and then at some point of time, when threatening with the trident, the retiarius would allow himself to be disarmed. From that point, the bout would continue unprepared, with unexpected movements, the victory going to the one who score the first "mortal blow."

"M. Dubois, armed only with his net, eventually secured a hold upon M. del-Prat and made as if to stab him, thus demonstrating his mastery of this phase of the exercise.

"However M. del Prat, foregoing his shield and relying upon the length of his sword, succeeded in seizing the edge of the net, and with all his strength he pulled the retiarius towards him. Surrendering the net would have been a terrible mistake on behalf of M. Dubois; instead, he yanked at the net from the side, forcing his adversary to hold on to the net with both hands, and therefore to keep his sword pointed upwards.

"While pulling, the retiarius released the net from his right hand, seized the dagger hanging from his belt and sprang towards M. del Prat, "killing" him with the dagger.

"This was, without doubt, a remarkable and very interesting form of combat, worthy of all encouragement!

"The equipment need not be expensive: a net, a simple wooden shield, sword and dagger, a fencing mask for a helmet, and a bamboo pole with a padded tip as a trident, are the only necessary accessories.

"However, we could only truly praise the sportsmen who would combine, with the recreation of this kind of contest, an accurate reconstruction of the gladiators' armament; that exhibition could not help but be more colourful and interesting.

"The unexpected reversals of fortune, the variety of movements of the combat, requiring the use of the entire body in a form of clever gymnastics, will undoubtedly seduce many aficionados who will want to follow the example set by Mssrs. Dubois and del-Prat, and spread these very intriguing reconstructions.

"In all of these exhibitions of ancient fencing, there is for the audience a scenic aspect that can be defined in two ways: firstly, as 'armed dialogues' and secondly as bold entertainments in which the fencers try hard to reconstruct a historic combat with the appropriate costumes, weapons, rituals and attitudes of the time.

"It is, in a way, a special kind of drama, all about action, whose outcome is sometimes uncertain since it depends on the fencing skills of the 'actors'; and perhaps by becoming more numerous, these contests will impart to true actors the enjoyment of fencing, which they too often neglect in their interpretation of heroic plays, which can then return with a new splendor, and be in vogue again. Rostand proved it with Cyrano de Bergerac, the eloquent hero, the champion of honour, the spiritual incarnation of the true French courage."

In 1908 George Dubois again represented France at the London Olympic Games. Competing in the 400-metre hurdle event, he suffered a leg injury that forced him to withdraw three-quarters of the way into his first race. Though disappointed, he stayed on in London to encourage his teammates.

At about this time, and for many years thereafter, Dubois was engaged as a fight choreographer for the Opera Comique in Paris. His insistence upon careful research and the practical testing of theory perfectly matched what his colleague, M. Albert Carre, described as a "hunger for truth in drama":

"The trend towards natural manners in acting and speaking was matched by the desire for exact authenticity in costumes, sets, and indeed in the execution of the least movement upon the stage. Clever reconstructions are now in vogue, and the director's library must be full of works on each era and each country if he doesn't want to miss out.

"However, we cannot demand such authenticity unless we allow him to appoint, in some cases, a specialist or professional with whom to collaborate.

"So it was at the Opera Comique, that they had a real Gypsy come from Seville, responsible for teaching Carmen and her friends the secrets of Flamenca; authentic Fadango dancers came in to teach the national Basque dance in *Chiquito*; a famous Japanese actress, Mme. Hanako, who was then passing through Paris, agreed to initiate Marguerite Carre, who was practicing for the role of Mme. Butterfly, into the ways of walking, sitting, saluting and of performing the hara-kiri; and to stage the knife-fight in *Leone,* a play set in Corsica, they did not fear to hire a real thief, who had killed a man, lived for five years in the forest, and, having obtained his pardon, now lives in peace in Bois-Colombes. He taught M. Snes, the creator of Leone, the manner to hold a knife and to dig it properly into his opponent's side, in 'the right spot,' as said the ex-criminal, smiling at the thought of it.

"But if it's about a combat with might and main, my lords, if it's about a duel with a sword, a dagger, a rapier, a spear, a knight's sword, a pirate's saber, a yagatan, an Oriental scimitar, a French duelling sword, a joust, a tournament, a fencing match in the French, Spanish or Italian styles, a bout between gladiators or wrestlers in ancient Rome, you must call in master Georges Dubois."

– *L'Escrime au Theatre: Rapiere et Dague,* 1910

The quote above is excerpted from M. Carre's introduction to Dubois' first book. *L'Escrime au Theatre* was a careful exposition of his syncretic approach to "artistic archeology." Although written primarily as a manual of rapier and dagger fencing applied to stage combat, the book also clearly demonstrates Dubois' eclecticism and pragmatic, methodical analysis of his weapons and their capabilities. The book is also noteworthy for some of its display advertising, which includes notices for two Parisian craftsmen who were producing replica weapons and armour for the study of *escrime ancienne.*

It was also in 1910 that Georges Dubois finally won an Olympic medal, although it was awarded for his artistic, rather than athletic talent.

His design for an "architectural statue" of the Olympic Stadium won the silver medal in an art competition attached to the 1912 Games in Stockholm, Sweden.

For the next several years, Dubois continued to combine his interests in the fine arts, the performing arts and the martial arts. In 1916 he produced another book, *Comment se Defendre,* presenting a notably realistic fusion of Japanese and French self-defence techniques. His daughter, Mathilde, played the role of the defender in several of the book's forty-eight instructional photographs. In the same year, Dubois also commenced a project of teaching fencing to visually impaired men, many of whom had lost their sight in battle during the War. His innovative system, which relied on a specialized set of exercises to develop his students' sense of *sentiment de fer,* was glossed in number of journals, including the May issue of the American *Popular Science* magazine.

Two years later, Dubois published his "Essai sur le traité d'escrime de Saint-Didier, publié en 1573," a brief but insightful analysis of the rapier fencing text produced by the 16th-century master-at-arms, Henri de Saint-Didier.

Rapier fencing was obviously one of Dubois' most intense interests. He was particularly intrigued by the rapier and dagger combination, arguing that the ambidexterity required in fencing with double weapons was beneficial both in terms of physical culture, because it encouraged a more symmetrical muscular development, and also in terms of intellectual engagement. During this period he was collaborating with another French fencing master, Albert Lacaze, who shared Dubois' interest in historical fencing techniques.

In 1925 Dubois published a further work on rapier and dagger fencing. *Essai sur l'Escrime: Dague et Rapiere* is particularly interesting by way of contrast to *L'Escrime au Theatre,* which had been published some fifteen years earlier. *Dague et Rapiere* was not a book of stage combat techniques, but rather presented an innovative system of artistic/competitive fencing with double weapons.

Introducing his own work, Dubois explains that:

> "Employing Fifteenth and Sixteenth century fencing terms creates something of a complication for the modern reader. A didactic book should present all of its explanations as clearly

as possible. Therefore I shall employ, in this essay on ancient fencing, terms that are familiar to masters-at-arms and to their students at the foil and epee, using the classical grammar of the modern French school.

"Moreover, I would appreciate it if the reader would adopt my conviction—based on studies within the historical oeuvre that even if the terms employed by the old Masters are not the same ones that we use today, then the methods that they described are as our own; they taught many of the same skills, since the guard of the sword was furnished with transverse branches that we all utilise scientifically.

"Thibault, of Anvers (1628) described this technique as requiring a particularly long period of study. He also wrote that the counter-riposte was a relatively recent invention. That was an error—Saint-Didier (1573) described it clearly, and supported his description with figures. Likewise, the development such as we conceive it, is clearly shown in Fabris (1606), as I shall demonstrate. Without hesitation or fear of committing any anachronism, we can assert that the historical Masters did require the traditional development."

Thus, in *Dague et Rapiere*, Dubois presents a historically-inspired double-weapon fencing system intended to complement the classical foil and epee fencing of his own era. He wrote that the system was based soundly upon the mutual study, by himself and Master Lacaze, of their collective fencing libraries, which included the works of Thibault, Capo Ferro and Fabris. In several respects it is very much the type of manual that Captain Hutton might have produced on this subject, had he been inclined to popularise reacreational "ancient swordplay" beyond his own small clique.

In October of 1927, the Pathe film company recorded an outdoor training session in the method of double-weapon fencing described in *Dague et Rapiere*. The footage was then edited into a silent newsreel item entitled *Fence and Keep Fit!*, which runs for a little over three minutes.

The newsreel begins with two boys wearing white shirts, sashes, black knee-breeches and stockings leading a group of ten others, similarly attired except that they are wearing light-coloured shorts, in a series of drills. Perhaps the black knee-breeches were worn by senior students. There follows a cue-card reading, "Fence and keep fit is a good saying here, for almost every muscle is brought into play in this double-handed sport."

The next two shots show individual boys (the first wearing black breeches, the second in all-white) demonstrating attitudes of defence and attack with their epees and daggers. Although the film is silent, they are evidently responding to the commands of an instructor, who remains largely out of the camera frame.

The fourth and fifth shots shows one of the youths in black breeches demonstrating an ambidextrous parry-riposte drill with a man wearing a light-coloured fencing jacket and breeches—this may have been Albert Lacaze. Their movements are swift and elegant.

Then appears a second cue-card, reading "A little more serious 'play' by the experts (slowed)." The final shot is in slow motion and shows the same man in the light coloured jacket free-fencing with a powerfully built older man in a black fencing master's uniform. This may well be Georges Dubois; although the film footage is not perfectly clear, the resemblance is very strong. Neither man is wearing a fencing mask, so it is likely that they were not fencing with full intent.

In 1934, another film crew visited the Salle Lacaze to record a visit by the famous Italian fencer Aldo Nadi. The same man in the light-coloured fencing jacket who was featured in the 1927 Pathe newsreel item is seen instructing a group of three young men wearing white shirts, sashes and black knee-breeches; perhaps some of them were also among those featured in the 1927 newsreel. The youths execute an elaborate salute and then a lunge with the epee and dagger.

The next shot shows a class of about twelve people at foil practice, including men, a woman wearing all black and two girls in white fencing jackets and black skirts. Aldo Nadi is then shown performing some controlled epee and dagger fencing with a student. The fourth shot returns to the group foil class, and then the fifth and final shot shows Nadi decisively winning a fast epee and dagger bout.

That same year, George Dubois died at the age of sixty-nine. Through his books and essays, historical fencing displays and theatrical fight choreography, he had been at the centre of the *escrime ancienne* movement for three decades. It was largely through his efforts, and latterly those of his colleague, Master Albert Lacaze, that the work begun by Alfred Hutton, Egerton Castle and their peers was perpetuated into the new century.

By this time, however, the clouds of conflict were again starting to cast their shadows over much of the world. Those martial pursuits that could have a practical application in times of war were unceremoniously appropriated from the realms of healthy recreation and scholarly knowledge and melted into the vast uniformity of training manuals for soldiers or future soldiers. Those that couldn't were cast aside.

A decade later, the Western world emerged an older, cynical, and conflict-weary place. Rebuilding a new life, a new economy and a new international conscience became the pursuit of most post-war nations, as men and women melancholically cleared the rubble of a world that was never again to be. For many people, the ideals, symbolism and practices of swordplay had been tainted by the fanaticism of lunatic regimes. During these confused times, an interest in historical fencing was often seen as distasteful or even politically suspect.

Thus, the task of re-discovery of ancient swordplay and the work of its pioneering authors awaited a new generation. As the 20th century drew to a close, rivulets of interest in these arts began swelling into a river, and new minds began devoting themselves to the study of centuries-old fighting arts. And whether or not the new scholars' conclusions matched those of Castle, Hutton, Dubois and their contemporaries, it did not matter—for these would be but disagreements among long-lost friends.

What mattered was that the arts were once again being brought back to life.

Gallery

The Joust between the Lord of the Tournament and the Knight of the Red Rose: an artist's impression of mounted combat at the Eglinton Tournament.

The Ex Libris book seal of Egerton Castle.

The late 19th century saw a revival of quarterstaff fencing amongst military men and in the Boy Scouts.

Professor Johann Hartl's Viennese Fencing Women pose with foils and daggers.

Dramatic performances by Hartl's ladies of the sword.

David Legault

A display of rapier and dagger combat staged by Legault
for a Canadian "Medieval Festival."

A bizarre "joust on foot" arranged by Legault for the same festival

Men and their toys: A night at the Kernoozer's club.

THE ILLUSTRATED LONDON NEWS, March 7, 1891.— 304

1. Mr. Egerton Castle reading his Paper.
2. Two-hand swords—Mr. E. Castle and Captain A. Hutton.
3. Italian sword and dagger v. English sword and buckler—Mr. Walter Pollock and Captain Hutton.
4. One of the parries.
5. Sword and cloak—Mr. E. Castle and Sir Fred. Pollock.
6. A practice on the mysterious circle—Mr. E. Castle and Captain Hutton.
7. Eighteenth-century small-sword play—Mr. E. Castle and Professor de Bailly.

a. Two-handed sword.
b. Italian rapier, sixteenth century
c. Spanish rapier, seventeenth century.
d. German sword, middle sixteenth century.
e. Italian rapier, third quarter sixteenth century.
f. Silver-hilted colichemarde, time William III.
g. Small sword, time Louis XV.
h. Shell dagger, sixteenth century.
i. Claymore, middle seventeenth century.
j. Hand buckler.

A LECTURE ON FENCING AT THE LYCEUM THEATRE.

"A Lecture on Fencing" – March 7th, 1891

Bibliophile and historical fencer Carl A. Thimm.

Blindfold lesson with foils. (modern).

"Preparing for a spring"

"Netted"

Four illustrations from an anonymous article entitled "Swordsmanship at the Merchant Taylor's School," in the November 10, 1894 *Black and White Budget* Magazine.

The more erudite side of "kernoozing" was a chief contributor in the serious study of arms and amrour in the late 19th century. The illustration is from the *Black and White Budget Magazine*, March [illegible], 1891.

Moments from Hutton's exhibition at the Windsor Cavalry Barracks, as recorded by the *Pall Mall Gazette* (May 2, 1893).

BOUT WITH TWO-HANDED SWORDS BETWEEN MR. CASTLE AND CAPTAIN HUTTON

EIGHTEENTH CENTURY SMALLSWORD PLAY BETWEEN MR. CASTLE AND PROFESSOR VITAL LE BAILLY :—DISARMED!

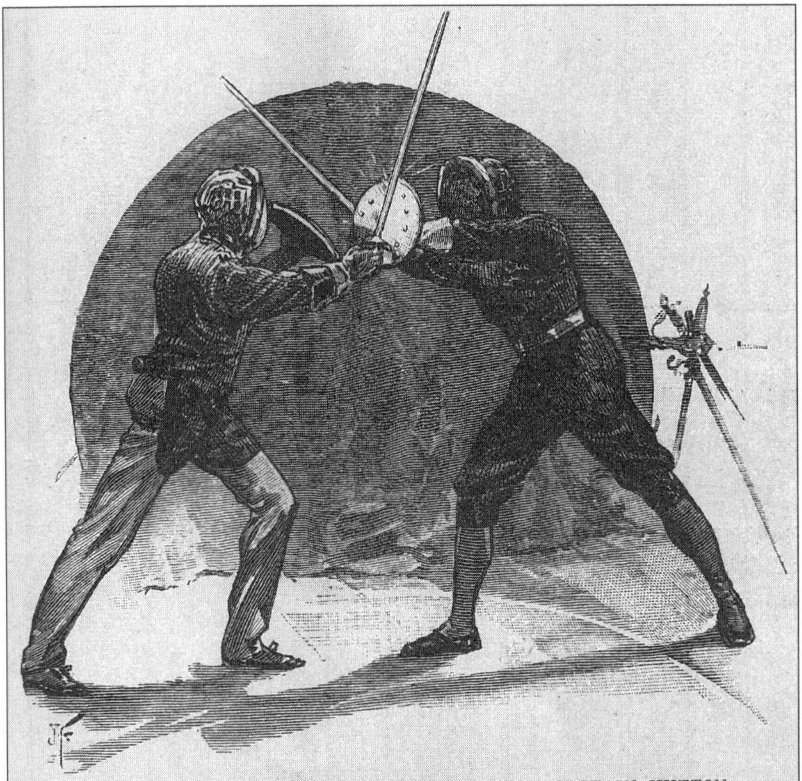

BOUT WITH SWORD AND BUCKLER BETWEEN CAPTAIN HUTTON AND DR. BIGGS

A FREE BOUT WITH RAPIER AND DAGGER

Five illustrations from the March 7, 1891 *Black and White Budget Magazine,* featuring Egerton Castle, Alfred Hutton, Vital Le Bailly, Dr. Mount-Biggs, and Frederick Pollock.

"Children playing with swords": the scene at the Windsor Cavalry Barracks following Hutton's display, from the *Pall Mall Gazette* (May 2, 1893).

Demonstrations of 17th-century smallsword and two-handed sword versus sword and shield fencing at the "Fete de l'Epee" exhibition, 1894.

Capt. Hutton and Egerton Castle exchange blows with the two-handed sword in a public display.

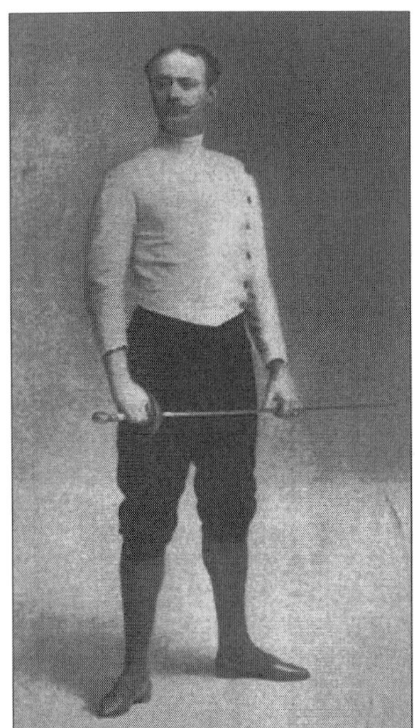

Hutton's conspirators: Egerton Castle in 1899, Captain Cyril Matthey posing with a cup-hilt rapier, circa 1898, and Edward William Barton-Wright, the founder of Bartitsu.

Actress and swordswoman Esme Beringer poses with two of her favorite weapons.

Esme Beringer displaying a crossed parry with rapier and dagger

A series of photos accompanying George Pollock's article "Rapier and Dagger Play" from *Country Life* magazine (May 17, 1902).

American Fred Gilbert Blakeslee demonstrates the use of various ancient weapons in his book *Sword-Play for Actors* (1905). Unfortunately, Blakeslee's efforts to bring the revival of historical swordplay to the States did not bear fruit.

ESMÉ BERINGER.

Did you see her performance at the Palace — one of the most sensational feats of swordsmanship ever seen on the stage? Miss Beringer, who is among the finest lady fencers living, learned the art mainly from Captain Alfred Hutton, a gentleman known in military circles as "Cold Steel," and also from Mr. Egerton Castle, the well-known novelist. Her performance was not altogether unattended with danger, for although the weapons are comparatively blunt, they are capable of inflicting nasty gashes. "But then," said Miss Beringer, "one suffers so much for first-night performances, that a mere sword-cut becomes quite a matter of indifference."

An early 20th-century playbill, asserting Eseme Beringer's bonafides as a swordswoman and pupil of Hutton and Castle.

Esme Beringer and George Silver (prone) in a scene from *At the Point of the Sword* at the Palace Theatre

Although he would outlive the considerably older Hutton, Egerton Castle ultimately chose the pen over the sword, leaving his later exploits with the rapier and dagger to the pages of his popular romances.

Performers from the Monnaie historical fencing festival display costumes and weapons from a range of eras.

George Dubois and Morris del-Prat demonstrate a reconstruction of gladiatorial combat, the first of its kind. Dubois' precise method of researching antique fighting arts was a clear forerunner to the "practical archaeology" of today.

Photos from Duboi's *L'escrime au théâtre: rapière et dague*

The immortal Cold Steel: Alfred Hutton as he'd no doubt prefer to be remembered, striking a fierce pose, weapons in hand. A pen and ink illustration, likely from his 1892 display for the Oxford University Fencing Club.

Appendix

Acknowledging the cultural devastations wrought by the Great Depression and then World War Two, it is still possible to trace historical fencing lineages in France throughout the 20th century.

Other than purely academic interest, the most practical application of historical fencing was understood to be in the world of theatre and film production. It was a matter of long-standing tradition that fencing masters should be employed to stage sword fight sequences and to train student actors in drama schools. As the work of Georges Dubois and Albert Lacaze was absorbed, to varying extents, within the sizeable French fencing infrastructure, the ability to offer historically-inspired swordplay became a marketable skill within the theatre and then film and television industries. So emerged the discipline of *escrime de spectacle* ("spectacular fencing").

As we have seen, Albert Lacaze's school was offering classes in epee and dagger fencing, directly inspired by historical rapier and dagger styles, into the early 1930s. According to fencer and fight choreographer Richard Alvarez, Robert Heddle-Roboth, who was formerly one of Lacaze's assistants, was still teaching a similar style of double-weapon fencing in Paris during the 1970s. Heddle-Roboth referred to this style as *escrime ancienne* (antique fencing). His most famous student was Marcel Marceau, who paid tribute to his teacher by remarking that Heddle-Roboth was "the Three

Musketeers in one man." It is likely that other French fencing coaches made greater or lesser reference to historical sources, supplemented by their own experiments with historical weaponry and their own imaginations as well, during this period.

Three of Albert Lacaze's assistants (his son Pierre, Robert Heddle-Roboth and Claude Carliez) went on to become senior figures in French fencing, and all three made particular specialties of historically-inspired theatrical swordplay. In 1990, Carliez proposed the new competitive discipline of *escrime artistique* (artistic fencing), based partially upon the model of competitive ice-skating. In *escrime artistique* tournaments, fencers would compete, not one-on-one as athletes, but rather in teams of two and more, performing elaborately choreographed fight scenes. Points would be awarded for imagination, costuming, fencing style and panache, although not for historical accuracy per se.

Since that time, *escrime artistique* competitions have burgeoned in popularity and they are now major events in the French, Italian and German fencing calendars.

Selected Bibliography and Further Reading

Allanson-Winn, R.G. and Phillipps-Wolley, C. (1890). *Broadsword and Singlestick – with Chapters on Quarter-staff, Bayonet, Cudgel, Shillalah, Walking Stick, Umbrella and other Weapons of Self Defence*. London, All England Series

Anglo, S. (2008). *Fencing or Fighting? George Silver, Cyril Matthey, and the Infantry Sword Exercise of 1895: Rediscovering an Elizabethan Swordsman in Late Victorian England*. Boulder, Paladin Press.

Armstrong, William (1902). *"Egerton Castle" The Book Buyer: a review and record of current literature*. London, Charles Scribner's Sons.Beaumont, C. L. de (1950). *Modern British Fencing: a history of the Amateur Fencing Association of Great Britain*. London, Hutchinson.

Blakeslee, F.G. (1905). *Sword-Play for Actors: a Manual of Stage Fencing*. New York, M.W. Hazen.

Cass, E.B. (1930). *The Book of Fencing*. Boston, Lothrop, Lee and Shepard Co.

Castle, E. (1892). *English Book-Plates: an illustrated handbook for students of ex-libris*. London and New York, G. Bell.

———. (1884). *Schools and Masters of Fence, from the Middle Ages to the Eighteenth Century*. London, Bell & Sons.

Clements, John. *Historical Fencing Studies – the British Legacy*. http://www.thearma.org/essays/BritLegacy.htm

Dreyer, J. C. H. (1754). *Anmerckung von den ehemaligen gerichtlichen Duellgesetzen, und von einem seltenen und unbekannten Codice, vorinnen des Talhoefers Kamp-Recht befindlich. Sammlung vermischter Abhanlungen zur Erläuterung der teutschen Rechten und Alterhuemer, wie auch der Critic und Historie*. Rostock.

Dubois, G. (1910). *L'Escrime au théâtre. Rapière et dague, avant-propos de M. Albert Carré*. Paris.

———. (n.d., circa 1916). *Comment se Defendre*. Paris, Nilsson.

———. (1918). *Essai sur le traité d'escrime de Saint-Didier, publié en 1573*. Paris, Chartres.

———. (1925). *Essai sur l'Escrime (Dague et Rapiere)*. Paris, Souzy.

Foster, F. (1875). "A List of Works on Sword Play." *Notes and Queries ser. 5* (no. 4): 201–2, 242–43, 262–64, 303–4, 341–43.

Goudourville, H. de (1899). *Escrimeurs Contemporains*. Paris, Chamuel.

Hergsell, G. (1881). *Die Fechtkunst*. Wien, Leipzig.

———. (1887). *Talhoffers Fechtbuch aus dem jahre 1467*. Prague, J.G. Calve.

———. (1889a). *Talhoffers Fechtbuch (Gothaer Codex) aus dem Jahre 1443*. Prague, author.

———. (1889b). *Talhoffers Fechbuch (Ambraser Codex) aus dem Jahre 1459*. Prague, author.

———. (1890). *Livre d'escrime de Talhoffer (manuscrit d'Ambras) de l'an 1459*. Prague, author.

———. (1893). *Livre d'escrime de Talhoffer (Codex de Gotha) de l'an 1443*. Prague, author.

———. (1894). *Livre d'escrime de Talhoffer de l'an 1467*. Prague, J.G. Calve.

———. (1896). *Die Fechtkunst im XV. und XVI Jahrhundert.* Prague OR Leipzig, Carl Bellman.

Hutton, A. (1862). *Swordsmanship. Written for the members of the Cameron Fencing Club.* 8vo. Simla: Simla Advertiser Press.

———. (1867). *Swordsmanship and Bayonet-fencing.* 8vo. London: W. Clowes & Sons.

———. (1882). *The Cavalry Swordsman. Bayonet fencing and sword practice.* 8vo. London: W. Clowes & Sons.

———. (1888). *Cold Steel: a practical Treatise on the sabre, based on the old English backsword play of the eighteenth century, combined with the method of the modern Italian school. Also on various other weapons of the present day, including the short sword- bayonet and the constable's truncheon. Illustrated with numerous figures, and also with reproductions of engravings from masters of bygone years,* 8vo. London: W. Clowes & Sons.

———. (1892). *Old sword-play: the systems of fence in vogue during the XVIth, XVIIth, and XVIIIth centuries with lessons arranged from the works of various ancient masters.* London and New York, H. Grevel and B. Westermann.

———. (1898). *The Swordsman: A Manual of Fence and the Defence Against an Uncivilised Enemy.* London.

———. (1901). *The Sword and the Centuries or, Old Sword Days and Old Sword Ways.* London, Grant and Richards.

Letainturier-Fradin, G. (1898). *L'Escrime a Travers les Ages.* Paris, Charles DuPont.

———. (undated, circa 1903) *Le Théâtre Héroïque.* Paris, Flammarion.

Matthey, C. G. R. (editor, 1898). *The Works of George Silver: Comprising Paradoxes of Defence and Bref Instructions Vpon My Paradoxes of Defence.* London, Geo. Bell and Sons.

McCarthy, T.A. (1883). *Quarter-Staff. A practical manual.* London, Sonnenschein & Co.

Murero, H. (1922). *Fechten im Bild.* Stuttgart.

Pearall, R. L. (1882). "Some Observations on Judicial Duels, as practised in Germany." *Archaelogia or Miscellaneous tracts relating to antiquity,* published by the Society of Antiquaries in London 29: 348–361, plates XXXI–XXXV.

Petrov, Julia (2008). "Bits of Kernooze"; *Homosociality and antiquarianism in Britain,* 1880–1914. University of Leicester

Pollock, Sir Frederick (1883). *Forms and History of the Sword.* London.

Rodriguez, F. P. y (1887). *Estudios sobre la grandeza y decadencia de España.* Madrid.

Schlichtegroll, N. (1817). *Talhofer, ein Beytrag zur Literatur der gerichtlichen Zweykempfe im Mittelalter.* München.

Sieveking, A.F. (editor, 1904). *Worke for Cutlers.* London, C.J. Clay and Sons, Cambridge University Press.

Schmied-Kowarzik, J. & Kufahl, H. (1894). *Fechtbüchlein.* Leipzig, Philipp Reclam.

Spielmann, Marion Harry (1889). "Glimpses of Artist-Life VII: The Kernoozers Club." *The Magazine of Art,* Vol. 12. London, Cassell and Company.

Thimm, C. A. (1896). *A Complete Bibliography of Fencing and Duelling as Practised by All European Nations from the Middle Ages to the Present Day.* London and New York, The Bodley Head.

Vigeant, A. (1882). *La bibliographie de l'escrime ancienne et moderne.* Paris, Motteroz.

Wassmannsdorff, K. (1870). *Sechs Fechtschulen (d.i. Schau-und Preisfechten) der Marxbrüder und Federfechter aus den Jahren 1573 bis 1614; Nürnberger Fechtsulreime v.J. 1579 und Rösener's Gedicht*: Ehrentitel und Lobspruch der Fechtkunst v.J. 1589. Heidelberg, Karl Groos.

———. (1888). *Aufschlüsse über Fechthandschriften und gedruckte Fechtbücher des 16. und 17. Jahrhunderts in einer Besprechung von G. Hergsell: "Talhoffers Fechtbuch aus dem Jahre 1467."* Berlin, R. Gaertners Verlagsbuchhandlung.

———. (1890). *Turnen und Fechten in früheren Jahrhunderten.* Heidelberg.

Webb, Ida M. (1999). *The Challenge of Change in Physical Education*: Chelsea College of Physical Education. Routledge.

Williams, H. D. (1923). *The Walled City: a story of the criminal insane.* New York and London, Funk and Wagnalls Co.

Wilson, J.D. (1934). *The Manuscript of Shakespeare's Hamlet, and the Problems of its Transmission.* London and New York, Cambridge University Press.

Wise, A. (1968). *Weapons in the Theatre.* New York, Barnes and Noble.

Wolf, Tony. (2009). *A Terrific Combat!!! Theatrical Duels, Brawls and Battles, 1800–1920.* Lulu Press.

———. (editor, 2005, 2008). *The Bartitsu Compendium volumes I and II.* Lulu Press.